An Anthology of Poetry,

&

Faerie Wisdom

Faeries of the Dark Wood

Mary Ann Benbow

M.A.B.

1

ISBN: 9798836746919

DEDICATIONS

Thank you to the Facebook group,

Finding the Fae, Channeling the Sidhe.

My Family.

To Michael Ross, for his unstinting help and patience.

To my Sidhe guide and friend.

I am dedicating this book to bridging the realms of Faerie and our human realm.

For the healing of the world and for all of the broken people out there.

To a unified future built on trust and love.

Are you one of those bridges?

Naomi Niahi Ani

For centuries Mother Earth has been violated and robbed of the tools she needs to function. Crystals and gems placed there to provide her heartbeat have been torn out of her.

Minerals that are her heart's blood have been looted and stolen. Mines have been abandoned and left like gaping wounds in her belly.

People take from her and soon there will be nothing left to take. She lies broken and bleeding and nobody listens, nobody seems to care.

They are scared, they are worried, but most of all they are angry.

We have one last chance to help them repair things otherwise the earth's axle is set to tilt and the waters will rush in. We are already seeing this with an increase in Tsunamis and Tidal waves, Earthquakes, and Hurricanes. Time is running out for all of us.

There is no longer anytime to think or ponder, the time is now.

Now, because tomorrow will be too late.

My name is Gunrig and I am of the E-SI, what you call Sidhe and I am a Magi Priest. I have come among you to beseech you to hear our call and join us before it is too late.

Gunrig

Gunrig on the Homeless

Something like 280,000 is thought to be homeless in the United Kingdom alone today while an estimated 326,126 in America.

More than 150 Million worldwide and most of these are some of the world's richest countries.

Ask yourself how this can be, is this a fair and decent world to live in.

How do we explain that the countries with the least homeless are the poorer countries, who still live in communities and share what they have?

Only when we change will we understand that in reality there is no I. We are all interconnected, we have one heart centre that beats for us all. In hurting anyone we hurt ourselves.

Neglect of others is the neglect of ourselves and in killing each other we eventually destroy ourselves.

But even worse than this by our indifference we kill the very earth we live on. The soil that grows our food, the Oceans that respond to the song of the moon.

Now the world is facing a climate change, the temperature is warming.

And very soon the Northern Hemisphere will be experiencing droughts not just for days, but for years. Think about that.

This will be caused by the kickback of nature, a nature that is so out of sync with mother Earth that it no longer responds to the ancient codex that was built into its core at creation.

This is entirely the human condition. We have no homeless in faeries, and animals are never short of a bed to sleep in because they are still in tune with nature, but soon even their world will change.

In their confusion and fear they will lash out and those that we have tamed over the centuries such as pets will start to access their original code and become wild again. Right now, many people are living in your urban cities amongst these people because we also feel we need to experience it to help us understand humans better. In the past, we were thought to dwell only in the countryside and many of us did because we did not have the huge cities that you have today. But we have always been in Towns and Cities. Look at a blade of grass that sprouts up between paving slabs. Or the little yellow flower that you pull up and call weeds. How do you think they live and grow without us? They are just as precious to us as flowers growing in a stately home or gardens everywhere. Look more closely at them the next time you see them. They are also created by us.

Do you then think that I am lying?

I tell you that I do not, or that I make jokes to scare you.

To what purpose would I do this? We in E-SI have seen all of this and much more.

We come to warn you and give you one last chance to change what soon will be.

Channeled by myself from Gunrig, my Sidhe friend.

Who are the Sidhe

Legends tell us that they first set foot in Ireland by arriving in a mist from the air. Possibly some kind of spacecraft perhaps. Certainly, it was believed that they came from the heavens and not the earth.

Some others believe that they were the fallen angels that were cast out of heaven because they rebelled against God.

These opinions still rage on today with various theories being thrown around, they only serve to make their origins even more shrouded in mystery. My own personal belief after much study of them and the scriptures is that they are the angels that were cast out from heaven.

But that is only my opinion, you must reach your own conclusions.

7

Some theorists believe that they first landed in Denmark and stayed there for ten years before moving on to Scotland. They possibly lived there for seven years before moving once more to Ireland and staying there. Now of course their descendants the E-SI live all over the world.

In Ancient Greece for example, it speaks of a race of nomads known as the Pelasgians. Tribal in nature, they were seafarers who claimed that they were born from the teeth of the Cosmic snake Ophian and the Great Goddess Danu.

This document claimed that they actually came from Greece and after trying to overthrow the rulers of Greece and failing they fled to Denmark.

What is for certain is that the more we dig into this race the more confused we become.

Their name is pronounced as 'Hoooo De Dannan'.

Singing the children's home have been channeling a Sidhe male for four years now and have several messages from him to give out in this book. Most of them are concerns that are very close to me.

Singing the Children Home

One of the things that Gunrig and I have discussed is something he calls singing the children home. Many children the world over have been taken and murdered. I wish that I had a nicer way to soften it but the truth is what has happened to them is very ugly. These babies are lost, truly lost in a black hole of fear and despair. The Sidhe can hear them but because they are human children they can't interfere. They ask that we sing them home. Set time aside to concentrate on them. Chant or beat a drum, please make some noise that could imitate a heartbeat. Set time aside even though your lives are busy and please sing them home.

I have to be brutal with you, just as he was brutal with me. There is no nice way to speak of it. These babies, maybe millions of them over time, were tossed away like rubbish. Their spirits are trapped by their bodies and they do not know what to do, so they wait there for someone to find them. Can you imagine the toxicity that is suffocating and poisoning our planet?

He has told me that by creating a vibration that mimics a heartbeat these poor babies will remember being in the womb, remember their mother and their spirit and will rise up to look for her.

This will then enable the Sidhe to gather them up and give healing and then get them home.

Please pass this on to friends and family. All you have to do is quietly meditate on these babies and then hum or drum as often as you can. This will not only release the spirits of these children but it will also remove so much toxicity from the earth.

These are the words of my Sidhe Guide as given to me.

Faerie Abduction

Faerie abductions are well documented in the Principality of Wales. One eyewitness account was disclosed by Mr. Pennant in a Faerie history of Holywell. Wales, 1792

He starts his statement by disclosing that on his land is a large faery mound and on the top of it is an ancient Oaktree. It is this Oak tree where the trouble seems to have begun.

Over the years many strange things had been seen here including lights, music playing, and lot's of noise and commotion.

One night a poor cottager went to look for the village midwife as his young wife was in labour. The cottager claims that he became Pixie mazed and was being led round and around in circles. Several hours had passed when a faery man appeared to him and asked him what his trouble was.

On learning that a new baby was about to be born the Faery man immediately offered his own service.

The cottager, who was by now frantic to get back to his wife, agreed.

So off they set.

On entering the house, the wife seeing the Faerie man became quite frantic, refusing to let her near him.

The Faerie man then started to sing to her in a beautiful voice.

Whether it was the song or the words he sang no one is sure, but the wife calmed down and the poor cottager wiped his brow.

Very soon the cry of a baby was heard and it was at this exact time that our friend Mr. Pennant should be passing and hearing such beautiful singing stopped by to see who it was.

Waiting outside in the cool night air, both men waited patiently.

Mr. Pennant congratulating the singer and secretly hoping that he could hire him to sing at his summer ball.

Our poor cottager just wanted to see his dear wife and his baby.

They waited for a long time.

Just as dawn was waking up both men had had enough of waiting, so opening the door, they burst in.

On the table was a pile of Faerie gold, a meal simmering on the fire, but of his wife and baby, there was no sign?

He thought he saw her once on a night when the moon was high. She rode past on a black horse with other riders turning her head just once to look at him.

This is just one of the numerous reported abductions to come out of Wales. Another one involved a young wife who one day went to the market to sell her butter and cheese. She was approached by a fine young man, handsome and clever, with a smile on his face and charm on his tongue.

The wife had seen him at the market several times so she smiled and inclined her head towards him

He was selling fruit, the most beautiful luscious fruit, and berries that were fat and ripe. The young wife desperately wanted some but knew her husband would beat her if she spent even a penny of the money she had made.

Eventually, the young man came over to her with a bowl of apricots and told her to take them as a gift. Though she wanted one desperately, she refused. She had been strictly brought up and knew she should not take gifts from men, other than her husband or her father.

The young man said he would accept a piece of her cheese as a fair exchange. She agreed to this and so she gave him a piece of cheese and he gave her the apricots. As she bit into the first one the juice dribbled down her chin. She sighed with delight, turning to the young man she had a surprise. He had fine ginger whiskers sprouting from the side of his face. She ate another one, again she closed her eyes and savoured the fruit.

The next time she opened her eyes the young man had two very pointed ears?

Realising that something was very wrong here she decided she would eat just one more apricot and then hurry home as fast as she could. This apricot was the best of all and when she tasted it she immediately stuffed the rest of it into her mouth.

When she opened her eyes, the market was full of grinning cats, dressed in fine waistcoats and pantaloons. Polished shoes and silk cravats.

The young man took her by the hand and started to dance with her. She was powerless to resist him and they danced faster and faster, around in circles until they were spinning so fast that they simply disappeared from sight. No one ever saw either of them again.

Why the Faeries left us.

Once upon a time a long time ago, or maybe it was yesterday, sometimes it's hard to know that Faeries lived alongside us and while we might not have been friends we were neighbours. We even referred to them as the good neighbours, but then we had a war and they moved away deep into the dark woods, wells, and caves and tried to ignore us.

The world became a darker place without their colour and laughter and in time, many of us forgot them.

Those that did remember were teased and laughed at for still believing in magic.

But now fear has instigated the Fae to return to walk amongst us. They seek out those of us who never forgot them, those who still honour them, and those who are willing to serve as a bridge between our realm and theirs.

Many aeons ago when the planet was very young and everything was new our brains were very different from what they are now. We had what has become known as ancient brains.

We were all much more primal then and even speech was not much more than noise, so our brain was designed to communicate through telepathy.

It was so well defined that we could smell far better than what we can do now. Hear much better and even see far into the distance. We relied on instinct.

We could communicate with others who shared our planet.

Over time while Faerie kept these communication methods, we humans moved further and further into matter. Over time our brains changed and developed into what we have now. Some of us however retained this ancient part of the brain and it sits now behind the left and right brains that we all have. It is this brain that allows us to communicate and even see Fae. It allows us to work and be involved with realms that others have no means to access. And it is people with this third part of the brain that the Aos Sidhe are seeking. To work with them in partnership to heal and save our world before it is too late.

Do we all have this remnant from our ancient past?

No, I don't believe that we do. But many of us do and I also believe that it can be reignited if we are prepared to put the work in.

Meditation to re-ignite the ancient brain.

This exercise is very similar to that of the yoga practice of raising the Kundalini. I recommend doing this exercise straight from the shower and wrapped up in a large fluffy towel.

Make sure that you won't be disturbed, turn off your phone then in a warm place start by lying on your side. It is entirely up to you which side you choose but it will probably be the side that you sleep on. If this is a physical problem then you can lie on your back.

Focus now on the noise of your blood rushing in your ear. Imagine that it is a raging river. When you feel comfortable with this and you might need a few days before you feel comfortable with this

Next, you will need to take your pulse. Some are very strong and beat loudly but some like mine are hard to find. Eventually, you will need to take it at the same time as listening to the flow of blood in your ear. No rush, this is your exercise and it must be done at your own pace, no hurry.

The reason for this exercise is to help you access your own reality which you can then access at any time. What is the most important part of this exercise, now becomes not the sound of your pumping blood, but the silence between beats. Once you have achieved this and no one will say it is easy, you will have created your own portal by using your heartbeat.

Practice, practice, practice.

Now, using your imagination, visualise a door in between your heartbeats. You choose its colour and design, its style i.e. a Faerie door or a castle door, your choice.

Let your imagination run wild.

What do you think is behind the door?

A beautiful garden filled with small dancing faces, a castle with a tall handsome Sidhe mounted on horseback, a river where Naiads wait to greet you, or a forest filled with smiling Dryads.

This is your portal and you can go wherever you want to go. This will re-awaken your ancient brain because it will recognize itself and what it once could do. Unlike going through other portals and never knowing where you will arrive, this is yours alone and you can choose where you go.

This will not be achieved in a day or a month, but with regular practice, it will open that part of your brain for you.

Be certain you really want it activated though, because once it is, it will take millennia before you can turn it off again!

Mrs. Rosy Apple

When I was a child, whenever we visited the park, which was often during school holidays, there was a tiny little elderly woman who herself was as round as an apple. She had two very shiny red cheeks that seemed to glow. Her long grey hair was plaited and wound around her head and she would either stand on her doorstep or sit on the park bench and watch the children. Our children called her Mrs. Rosy apple.

She was married to the barkeeper who was small and round himself. With grey bushy eyebrows and a grey bushy beard..

She would move with agility if any of the children were hurt she would clean up the wound and give us all a piece of homemade toffee. She was also fierce in dealing with bullies. One day some boys arrived the thought that it was a good idea to turf us, girls, off the swings, Looking around them to see if Mrs. Rosy was about and it looking clear, they did the dastardly deed

Suddenly the swings started to move by themselves, they went higher and higher with the boys scared and yelling. One boy actually jumped off grazing his needs while his two friends hung on for dear life. Suddenly Mrs. Rosy appeared and the swings stopped suddenly. The boys ran off and I don't know if they ever came back.

Another strange thing was that nobody knew how old she was but my mother said she was there when she was a child.

The Faerie Lament

We spun the web and we tell the stories.

We sing the songs.

It was we, who made it so,

where are our friends, and our achievements?

Where do we come from?

Where do we go?

We tend the land, ours is the glory.

Where do we come from?

Where do we go?

We came from the mist,

is that where we return to?

Where do we come from?

Where do we go?

All those we loved and all those we feared,

our sunshine,

our laughter, all of our tears

The dew in the morning,

the sunshine or rain.

It was you who brought changes,

we stayed the same.

So where do we come from?

Where do we go?

The world that we live in made us so.

Meeting my Faerie Guide

Many people ask me how we met, my Sidhe and I, and I tell them it was while camping with friends four years ago on the beautiful mystical Isle of Skye on the west coast of Scotland and accessed by a road bridge that joins the Island to the mainland.

It is a place that I have always been fascinated with ever since I learned about Bonnie Prince Charlie and heard the Skye boat song for the first time.

An island of mystery, shrouded in mists and purple heather, legends, and of course, Faeries.

On only the second night at some time in the early morning I heard my name being called, "Evangeline," for one horrible moment in my drowsy state I thought it was my old headmistress, she was the only person to ever use my first name.

Trying to calm my thumping heart, I rationalised that surely she would be dead by now unless it was her ghost. But it sounded male?

My partner at the time was sound asleep aided by several bottles of Coors lager, so I peered out of the tent flap to see if anyone really was there!

Standing only a few feet from me stood a male figure, I am tall but he towered over me. He was the most handsome man that not only had I ever seen, but in my childish dreams, had ever existed.

His hair was black and he had round blue eyes without lids or lashes.

He simply held out his hands to me and without any hesitation, I walked into them...

I was aware of standing in a glow of bright light, at first I thought it was the moon but on our next meeting in daylight, I realised that the glow came from within him from his heart chakra.

Four years later I remember everything about that meeting but the day after it I thought it had been a dream and it faded as the day moved on as dreams usually do.

He wore a plain, white, blouson top and black leggings, that skimmed his thighs.

His feet were bare and his toes had small webbing between them, but it was his scent that really aroused me, he smelt of thick pinewoods, but something else?

Musk, but not musk that is used in perfumes. I actually dislike any perfume containing musk. The scent was unique to him and him alone. It is strange, but I have always been attracted to a man by his scent and I mean his real scent and not expensive aftershave, and by his hair. Clean, shiny hair, is a strong turn-on for me.

His touch set me on fire and he spent a long time just stroking my hands with his long pale fingers. All of the time staring into my eyes. I am now quite certain that he was fully aware of the reaction his touch had on me.

His fingers then moved to my hair and he ran his fingers through it then down to my neck then shoulders. The most ecstatic impulses coursed through me totally uncontrollable until I was practically whimpering with pleasure. Then he held me close until the sun peeped over the Scottish mountains, and then he was gone with no promise of returning.

Now that I know him much better that is the Faerie way. They don't make plans and they don't make promises, though they do make bargains of which we should all beware.

That was four years ago and we are still together. I don't ask him what he does when he is somewhere else and he doesn't ask me, what is important to both of us, I think, is what happens when we are together.

Faeries must always be free to go wherever they want to go and see whoever they want to see. They simply would not tolerate any kind of emotional dependence or jealousy. They don't understand it.

My Sidhe Lover

He walks toward me,

my Sidhe man.

His hair is as black as night.

His feet make no sound upon the soft

moss that he treads.

A wise old owl watches us

with interest.

His eyes, blue orbs, shine with love,

as they rest on me.

Pale hands with long cool fingers

touch my face.

His fingers part my lips and linger there.

He wears a cloak of forest green, held

in place of an oval gold.

His hair as long as mine rests gently on his

shoulders.

My Sidhe man makes no demands on me,

he asks for nothing that I do now willingly give.

Then the peace is broken as he starts to whistle.

A high keening sound.

The wise old owl joins in.

Then I start to whistle too and give him my answer.

Our hands clasp, his grip is cool and firm.

Yet one last time he asks me, "Are you sure?"

I smile and nod my head.

Together, forever, we walk into the mound.

Elves and the Huldafolk

Known as the hidden folk, Huldafolk, or Elves as they are known in Iceland live in nature in volcanic rock.

They look and behave very similar to ourselves with one exception.

These beings are breathtakingly beautiful and in general, at least are several inches taller than we are.

Because Iceland itself is a very mystical country being mostly erected up on powerful ley lines the people live quite openly among the Elvin folk and quite even marry.

A survey in 2006 showed that 54% of the Icelandic people believed in them.

Roads have been diverted after public protests complained that the original proposal would destroy Elven habitats.

Elves were mentioned in many skaldic verses, they were also mentioned in the Poetic Edda.

In one Christian folk tale, the origins of the hidden people can be traced back to Adam and Eve.

Eve hid her dirty, unwashed children from God, and lied about their existence.

God then thundered, "Whatever man hides from God, God will hide from man". So, they became the hidden people.

Good luck befriends thee, son, for at thy birth

the faery ladies danced upon the hearth.

Thy drowsy nurse has sworn she did them spie,

come tripping to the room where thou didst lie:

And sweetly singing round thy bed,

strow all their on thy sleeping head.

John Milton

A.E. George Russel, who was himself a very down-to-earth plain-speaking man wrote about Faeries in crowded rooms all over the world.

He describes a meeting he had with a Sidhe.

There was a dazzle of bright searing light, which I could see came directly from the heart of a tall figure with a body apparently shaped out of half-transparent or opalescent air. Throughout its body ran a radiant fire of which the heart was the centre.

Around the head of this being was waving luminous hair, like a flaming wing-like aura.

William Sharp (1855-1905)

Wrote under the pen name of Flora Macleod.

He seems to have fallen under an enchantment by Faeries after a strange encounter after a visitation from a luminous being described above.

He suddenly began to write wild plays and poetry about the shining ones.

The ancient Faerie race of the Celts.

How beautiful they are,
the lordly ones
Who dwell in the hills,
in the hollow hills.

They have faces like flowers,
and their breath is the wind
that blows over the grass.
Filled with dew clad clover.

Their limbs are more white
than shafts of moonshine.
They are more fleet
than the March wind.

They laugh and are glad,
and are terrible.
When their lances shake,
every green reed quivers.

How beautiful they are!
How beautiful!
The lordly ones,
in the hollow hill.

Faerie Myth or Truth

One of the gifts that we receive from Faeries is unconditional love.

A Faerie gift is a power, Faeries themselves are very powerful.

True power comes when we are able to activate our life force so that we change not only our own personal power but to be able to leave our imprint upon the world.

It is this gift that presents you with your magic wand.

If you do not want this gift then it is at this point you must say so because once accepted you will never be able to put it down.

This is a lifetime commitment both by you and by them.

See yourself standing in a great hall filled with Faeries of many different kinds.

Draw in your mind a circle around you of blue flames.

The Faerie queen approaches you and asks you if you will accept this gift?

Having done so, she also will step inside your ring and lightly touch you with her wand.

The effect is instantaneous. Your body becomes alive like it never has before.

Light flows from your body like fireworks shooting high into the sky.

A deep love engulfs you to the point of almost overwhelming you.

Look at your faery friends and notice the love and deep acceptance that they now include you in.

No longer are you a separate entity but a deep part of them.

You merge with them just as they merge with you.

Each is connected to the Gaia Earth vibration.

As this gift truly awakens and continues to grow in you, you realise that now you are genuinely connected to the energy of all life here upon the Earth.

This gift is your right and your Faerie heritage.

For anyone needing a financial boost, look at working with oils, candles, or cosmetics.

Make your own. I will share some recipes with you near the end of this book.

Along with making your own wand

Another of their gifts is 'Expression'.

So many of us find it hard to fully express ourselves.

Expressing yourselves includes accepting your own individuality.

Millions of pounds are spent today trying to look like a better version of ourselves.

Yet thousands of ancestral DNA has gone into your creation.

Faerie Sight

So much has been written in folklore about faerie sight.

From rubbing ointments into the eye, to bathing in marigold petals.

When the Faeries realise that they can be seen their revenge can be swift. People have been reportedly blinded or killed, but mostly they are taken to work as servants in the underworld.

But it is a different story that should be given to you.

This is a sign of trust and acceptance.

Here you stand in the same great hall.

Place the blue circle around you.

Once more the faerie queen approaches you and asks if you accept it?

At your acceptance, assuming that you do accept of course, she steps into the ring of blue fire with you.

Pointing her wand at your eyes she will ask you to close them.

As she gently touches your eyes with her wand you become aware of a myriad of beautiful colours in shades you have never seen before.

The colours become bubbles that encase you.

You find yourself standing in a bubble that rises up in the air.

Here the Faeries join you.

Also riding inside bubbles, they laugh when the bubbles burst.

Suddenly you are outside the hall and you are surrounded by trees. As your eyes adjust to the brightness of the light you see a small man dressed in brown, except for a red hat that sits jauntily on his head.

With thick white hair and a beard, he removes his hat and bows to you.

Tells you that his name is Aelfdene and he is the guardian of this forest kingdom.

By giving you his name, he is placing great trust in you.

After greeting you he begins to show you around his kingdom.

There are trees bending with the weight of ripe fruits and nuts.

Don't eat anything.

This is Faery food.

You can request a cup of water if you need it?

But eat or drink nothing else.

Removing your shoes, if you haven't already, then push your feet deep into the cool damp moss beneath you.

This is grounding yourself and is a safety net to keep you connected to the human world.

Because they will keep you if they can.

They have accepted you by now.

Trusted you by now and obviously like you, so keep you they will if they can.

In front of you is a lake of the clearest blue water and rowing a crystal boat towards you is a tall handsome Elf.

Healfdene helps you into the boat and you start to move across the water.

A huge old turtle swims past you with two Nyads on his back.

Silverfish jump high out of the water and land with a loud splash, creating ripples that spread out right across the lake.

Along the lake's grassy banks, you see Faerie children playing and picking flowers.

A mermaid pops her head out of the water to take a look at you.

Don't take her hand should she offer it.

Faerie land is beautiful beyond description, but it can be dangerous.

Just like ours can.

We have to follow the rules, just as we do here.

It would be a shame if you were scared off because of the dangers.

Just make sure you are equipped with the knowledge you need before you visit.

Soon you are returned to the shore where you are greeted once more by the forest guardian.

As you turn to thank him and say goodbye, you come back to yourself.

Rain in the Night

I missed you last night,

the ring of bright toadstools and daisies,

and clover went unused.

It is now looking windblown, are the words

that I use.

Its energy is gone and its enchantment,

all because we had rain at night.

Dancing in any form creates huge energy, but dancing round and round in a circle means that as the pace gathers, the energy it creates matches the energy of the planets that circle the world.

Remember that it is not just in your garden that they dance. Nor mine, they are dancing the world over.

A circle has no beginning, nor does it have an end.

A circle is equal and that is how they view the world.

What increases its power is the fact that while the stem reaches deep down in the soil, the cap reaches up to the stars

Never step inside a fairy ring because it's said that you will be stolen away to Faerie land and never be seen again. As they dance within the ring the mushrooms themselves can be used as stools for when they need to step out of the ring without actually breaking it.

The Power of Circles

We wear rings when we commit ourselves to one person. As children, we dance in rings despite no one ever telling us to.

Dogs chase their tails in circles.

Ripples on the water form circles, and puddles form into circles.

The moon culminates her transition into a circle.

Circles are both used as protection and as doorways.

It works from both without and within.

The outer barrier protects from outside intruders while the inside area safely contains the magic and energy that has been raised.

These circles are in fact a very sacred and magical place.

It contains several of the elements needed for creation. First is Earth, the physical one. The stems come from the Earth where it is centred.

Next, its cap reaches boldly up to the sky so it contains air.

Fire is a nod to their bright red colour, although I have seen circles where the toadstools have been white.

We are never too old for a Faerie story and I composed this one to read to my garden Faeries.

They loved it because they love a jest.

Try reading it aloud in your garden and see how they react.

The Story of Finbar Finegan

Once upon a Faery time, a long time ago,

or it might have been only yesterday,

these things are hard to know.

Finbar lived in a sweet little cottage, surrounded by daisies,

buttercups, and cows, in a green valley in Ireland

Finbar was a dreamer.

He liked to go for long walks in the hills.

He would often take off his shoes and stockings because he liked

the feel of the grass beneath his feet.

Then Finbar would fall asleep and dream of being rich and famous.

When he woke up the sun would be going down over the hillside.

So Finbar would hurry home to his wife and children often leaving

his shoes behind in a hurry.

One day Finbar's wife told him he must go out fishing as they had

nothing to eat.

Finbar clapped his hands happily for he liked a bit of fishing.

Finbar tells her that he would bring them back eight fine trout and

they would eat like kings.

Mrs. Finbar raises her eyes to heaven, knowing her husband as well

as she did, did not hold out much hope of eating anything but

potatoes, never mind fat trout.

On reaching the riverbank and finding a nice shady place out of the sun, Finbar sets up his rod and sits and waits.

And waited, but not a fat trout did he see.

Eventually, Finbar falls asleep.

The sun drops low and the air begins to cool down

When Finbar is awoken by a loud cry for help.

There, in the centre of the river, dressed so finely that he might have been a prince, was a Faery man.

Finbar jumped into the river and rescued the drowning man.

Safe on the bank the Faery man bows very courtly and declares that for saving his life he will grant him three wishes.

Being a man of simple taste and low ambition Finbar declares

"I wish for health!"

"Done!" cries the Faery King, you shall have it.

Finbar Finegan, you shall die as healthy as you are today.

Finbar tried to recall all of the Faery lore that he had learned from his Mammy.

I wish for a long and happy life he declares.

The Faery King smiled coldly.

"Then you shall have it," he cried.

Finbar Finnegan, I grant you 100 years to add to your span.

But you shall live it happily though hungry and alone.

Finbar scratched his head.

For certain these Faeries can be crafty folk.

"Be quick," the Faery King tells him, that I must be on my way.

I wish the lord that I had never drawn upon your power.

Indeed, I wish that I had never set my foot on Faery bower. So I wish my lord to leave this place exactly as I found it.

My life is unchanged.

The Faery King smiled this time with a smile that lit up his entire face.

Clasping Finbars hand, he declares,

"Three wishes you had,

but the third one set me free.

Your kindly act has filled my heart with glee,

I wish you health and wealth and more

And eight fat trout's are at your door".

With that, the Faery King vanished.

The setting off for home, he hoped

that the King spoke the truth.

But as he drew closer to this home, he heard his wife and children singing out for glee.

With eight, fat, brown trout's to eat for tea.

The Hawthorn Tree

He stands alone, and proud, guarding his kingdom.

He can't remember how long he has stood here,

or how many birthdays he never had.

When he was just planted,

the birds laughed at him.

Then the moles laughed at him.

"You are far too small to be a guardian," they said.

"We need a mighty oak.

Or even,

a beautiful Elm that can reach the sky".

But then the Faeries came and sat in his branches,

decorated him with fairy dust and kissed him.

Then the birds stopped laughing!

And the moles stopped laughing!

In fact, no one was laughing anymore,

Except for the Hawthorn tree!

Because he was beloved by the Faeries.

The Faery Procession

First, we heard the sound

of the Faery flutes.

Come softly on the wind,

a plaintive tune,

serenades the moon.

The Faerie folk are here.

Sometimes they come with the ring of

a bell.

Sometimes the drum beats loud!

Sometimes they sing,

and a bell they ring,

In a laughing dancing crowd.

And

And just like that, she was gone.

The girl I used to be, now in her place,

is a woman grown,

who was ever scared to walk alone, so,

gave her love carelessly.

Then one day she was shown,

that it's ok to walk alone,

along a faerie path.

Breath of air.

A land unknown

A magic place that she was shown.

Another life.

Another time.

A love enduring place and time,

Was how it was meant to be.

For me, poetry has always been a way of being able to express myself.

I struggled as a child and not only as a child with dyslexia and although I knew exactly what I wanted to say, it never came out that way. But I always loved writing. As a student when my classmates handed in one sheet of paper and maybe two from the swots, I would beamingly hand over eighteen. I now have a better understanding of why my teacher's face would fall, or her smile never reach her face.

"It was all there Evie!" she would tell me a week later, when she had finally worked her way through it.

Just not in the right order.

It was poetry that came to my rescue, because I could finally say in just a few words what it was that I wanted to say.

The Blackthorn Tree

Wake me when the Blackthorn blooms,

and put out my pretty shoes,

for my Sidhe love returns to me,

when the Blackthorn blooms.

He left me when the winds blew cold,

and my heart was filled with pain.

And I wept beneath the Blackthorn tree,

and my tears fell like rain,

but they fed the roots of the blackthorn tree

so that it would bloom again.

My Sidhe love and I dance under the moon,

And his kisses will be tender when the blackthorn blooms.

The blackthorn tree is beloved of the Faeries and they regularly hold their courts beneath them. Blackthorn is considered in Faery lore to be able to keep secrets.

Bridging the Faerie World

Throughout history, humans have tried to describe the Faerie realm in stories, songs, and paintings. Yet these can only ever be a shadow of the real thing simply because we have nothing that could remotely emulate what they had seen there.

We do not share their colour spectrum, we cannot listen as they talk together and we most certainly taste their food.

So no matter how hard we might try to explain it, the only real way to experience it is to see it for ourselves.

The land of Faerie is not simply visual, it has to be felt,

So, should we ever find ourselves there, one thing that can be taken as certain, is that it will be nothing like you have ever experienced before, and neither will it be what you expected?

The land of Fae will always be different for everyone because each of us is different?

Their world exists on vibration and the place you visit will be one that will be able to accommodate your vibration best.

These different worlds are home to different Faeries, this is why we have both Seelie and Unseelie courts.

Even the Seelie can have off days so even arriving at this high plain there is no guarantee that they will all be pleased to see you.

44

This is why I advise people to get in touch with their animal totem, then you can take them with you for protection.

I certainly would not want to visit the Unseelie court, but then for anyone on that low vibration would probably be right at home there.

However, this book is not about the Unseelie, but I already have ideas about writing on the faerie courts at a later date.

What can expect to see at the Seelie court?

Well, certainly Elves and Sidhe, that goes without saying.

Many elemental faces, though some renegade elementals are also at the Unseelie court.

Flower Faeries, Brownies, Divas, Nymphs, Dryads Mermaids, Unicorns, Fauns and Pixies, and this list is not extensive, there are many more that I haven't mentioned because I don't know all of them.

Besides these high vibration Faeries, you will also encounter, Titania and Oberon.

They are the Queen and King of the summer court.

Both are extremely tempestuous and have very fiery tempers.

While you are here it is quite possible that you will have a Faerie make a request of you in the way of favour, it is up to you how you respond, but my advice is to ask for time to think about it.

Never let yourself feel pressured into agreeing to do something and never give your word unless you are absolutely certain you can keep your promise. Because Faeries most definitely can bite.

They don't share our morals or ethics, and to them, everything is black or white, definitely no shades of grey where they are concerned. If you agree to do something then they expect you to do it. No excuses or unmitigated circumstances will ever be accepted.

Their own problem-solving skills are quite literal. For instance, if you were to ask for help cleaning up a riverbank, you are quite likely to hear of a spate of drownings. Their idea of solving the problem would be to eliminate the litterers.

Always be on your guard and never speak in haste.

Despite the risks involved, as long as you think before you speak then working with Faerie can be very rewarding.

Another thing you need to be aware of is that they are great tricksters and the joke will always be on you.

Faerie Bath Salts

When preparing for a Faerie ceremony or meditation, the bath salt recipe below will not only prepare you for being in the Faerie presence, but on a magical level it will make you feel alert and pampered. It also has the added benefit of being made by some of the Faerie's favourite flowers.

You will need a pretty glass jar:

Three parts Epsom salts.

Two parts baking soda.

One-part table salt.

A handful of dried garden or wild flowers.

Place everything in a large bowl and using a wooden spoon mix it all together.

Then place the combined flowers and salts into your jar and leave for three days in the sunlight and moonlight.

Thyme is a herb that is beloved by the Fae. It's pretty pink flowers and its wonderful smell attract them to the gardens and homes where it grows.

An old charm using thyme was found in an ancient grimoire that somehow ended up in auction here in the UK.

This is said to allow you to see into the world of the Fae, it includes the flowers and leaves of Thyme, Marigold flowers, rosewater and Hazel buds. Steep in the rosewater for seven days.

Lavender

This beautiful purple flower is also known as the Elf leaf. As the name suggests, it is believed to attract elves and also helps you see into the Fae world.

In Faerie lore, the little folk make lavender infused wine for their midnight parties. They also love the scent of this fragrant flower, so if you have a faerie garden this plant will ensure that you get plenty of Faerie visitors to it.

On a medical record, lavender has been used to treat migraines, rheumatism, nausea, colds, and can induce sleep.

The essential oil is also good for insect bites and stings. It can reduce stress and anxiety.

Magically lavender is used in many love spells and in rituals to bring happiness and peace, it also was burned on Midsummer's eve by being thrown into bonfires.

Sweet Woodruff

This lush herb with its delicate white flowers is used by the Faeries in their midnight revelries, as it reflects the moonlight and adds potent magic to a spell casting. This beautiful flower is aligned with the element of fire.

Growing it will encourage fire elements to visit your garden. Its high fragrance makes a beautiful ground cover.

Faery Powder

Creating a Faerie powder is very easy to do and it is an easy way to incorporate the magical property. The powder can be stored in a jar and used whenever you need to call on the faeries.

To see the Faeries, make a powder of one-part thyme, one-part lavender and one-part sweet woodruff.

Grind the required herbs in their dried state with a mortar and pestle, empowering them with energy and intent. Then sprinkle them on your altar.

Store it in a glass jar and use as needed.

Heather

This hardy plant with its small, pretty flowers, grows wild and abundant across moorlands and heaths of Europe and now increasingly in the Southern hemisphere as well.

Medically, heather can be used to treat gout, rheumatism, arthritis. It is good for treating eye infections, stomach aches and ulcers.

I really enjoy a cup of heather tea to start the day as a pick me up.

Magically, it's used for protection. A small heather plant is good to have in the home and in the garden. This plant is connected to the Goddess Bride and can be woven into Bride crosses to hang in the home and car.

Mint

Also known as monks herb, this is an important ingredient in Faerie drinks and Faerie food, and its heavenly scent and pretty flowers make it a must have in Faerie gardens.

Medicinally, it has long been used to aid digestion and stomach disorders, it can be used to treat sore throats in a mouthwash, colds, flu, asthma, colic and earache.

Marigold

I absolutely love their beautiful cheerful flowers and use it in my skincare products. This flower also attracts Faeries.

Also known as calendula, you can add its petals for cake decorations.

It has long been used in cooking.

This flower is used for divination, especially if you are looking for your soul mate.

Marigolds have long been planted on graves and burial sites to bless the dead and ensure peaceful sleep.

Medicinally they are excellent for any inflammatory disorder, such as eczema and psoriasis.

Chamomile

Chamomile is one of the mainstream herbs and its usage is various. Tea is widely available in supermarkets, but it is also very easy to make, by drying the flower heads, then letting them steep in boiling water.

This is without doubt a wonder herb, it soothes the nerves, calms the spirit and aids sleep.

Magically it is used for purification and protection. It can be used in the bath to prepare for a ritual, in incense and burners to encourage relaxation.

To entice the Faeries into your dreams, you can make a dream pillow.

Sew together two soft pieces of cloth, such as velvet or satin. Then mix a herbal blend of one part dried chamomile, one part dried rose petals, two parts milkweed, one part dried lavender, one part dried poppy flowers.

Place into your cushion and sew up the open end. This should last four to six months. Place it under your pillow.

Vervain

I absolutely adore this herb, the perfume that I wear is Vervain based, and I love not only how it smells, but how it makes me feel.

It is a small perennial plant with lilac flowers and is used in love potions and healing spells, and has long been considered sacred.

It is revered by druids, and priestesses as a protection herb.

It is used in initiation rites, to crown priestesses, invoking spirits and when added to water, it can be sprinkled on people as a blessing.

Roman priests used it thousands of years ago on their altars.

Today it is used by magical herbalists, to prevent bad dreams and to boost intuition.

Elecampane

Also known as elfwort, with its cheerful yellow flowers that look a bit like dandelions, it is closely associated with Elven magic, and will connect with the ancient earthy powers of Elven magic.

It can be used in love potions, and rituals, particularly if you are wanting to connect to Elven magic. The roots can be dried and scattered around the home to welcome the Faeries.

Used in rites of initiation and deep magic, the flowers can be worn or carried in a pocket to attract love.

Daisies

These cheerful little flowers are very easy to grow, and they represent love and sunshine. Wherever daisies grow there will be Faeries. They are a particular favourite of Dryads. These flowers aid communication. For many years these little flowers have been used in love divination. By pulling off the flower petals. "He loves me," "He loves me not."

Honeysuckle

This fragrant flower can be carried to help you forget a past love. It is also used to boost psychic powers and assist with divination, clairvoyance and psychic awareness. By simply crushing the flowers and rubbing them on your forehead and body before spell casting, or drying and adding them to a carrier oil such as sweet almond, you can create a magical oil for anointing yourself to increase abundance.

Growing honeysuckle in your garden is believed to attract wealth and abundance.

You can also place a bunch of fresh flowers in your home to attract abundance.

Faerie Stones

Faeries have long been associated with stones and crystals.

They can heal, protect and help concentration.

I always carry Amethyst with me and have it in my bedroom.

Amethyst, its other name is Bishop's stone.

Element Magic

The season of Faerieland, do not necessarily tie in with our own.

Chakras – The Third Eye

Traditionally, Amethyst has been used in the treatment of headaches and migraine, insomnia and bad dreams. It calms the mind and clears the third eye chakra.

It has also been used to help with addictions, depression and pain. Gentle but powerful amulets of this crystal have been used for centuries and it was very popular both in ancient Greece and with the Romans.

In Britain because of its purple colour, it is considered to be a royal stone and several very beautiful pieces are to be found in the crown jewels.

Amethyst is a crystal that is par excellence of the Faerie spiritual path or Faerie faith, as it is sometimes called. If you are serious about following this path, then I recommend that you get a piece of this crystal and keep it with you.

In Tibet, Amethyst is sacred to the Buddha.

For those of us of the Faerie faith, Amethyst, and the faeries who accompany it, are involved in protection spells, spirituality and magic.

Amethyst is the gemstone of sorceresses, shapeshifters, and the Faerie Queen. This gem encourages learning and when working with Fae it can be used against deception.

Elven Moonstone

This stone is usually grey with black spots, it might look a bit boring in comparison to other stones, but don't be fooled, this stone carries great power. It has very strong connections to Norway and the dark Elvin months of the northern lights . It got its reputation for aiding connection with elves after it was discovered in some abundance in places where elves were believed to live. This is the stone of the guardian and many people carry it with them for safety.

It can also be used in Elven magic to help manifest them and call them to you.

This stone also has strong links with the Norse Deities and this stone will hold huge appeal to you.

Fairy Cross Stone

This stone can be found from anywhere from Norway to Mexico, the most common place to find it is a place called Faerie stone park in Virginia, USA, which is named after these magical stones.

The legend behind it says that the Faeries when they heard about Christ's death wept tears and those tears turned into these stones.

Faerie cross stones are stones of compassion and signify coming together. If you want to connect with Fae energy, then this stone could help you to do it.

Moonstone

Moonstone comes in many colours, including white, peach, and grey, all have a milky sheen and a luminous opalescence.
This stone has strong connections to the Faerie ring and the Faerie dance and its vibration is suited to all those who like to dance.
Moonstone shows us our inner light and has strong connections to the Faerie world.
This stone is considered lucky, so it is a good stone to carry with you in your purse or wallet. It is also connected to the moon and the moon goddess, Cleo.

Hail to thee, thou new moon,
guiding jewel of gentleness.
I am bending my knee to thee,
I am offering my love to thee.

All Faeries adore Moonstone because it contains the power and energy of the full moon. Which they always celebrate with feasting and dancing.

It can also be carried as a Faerie talisman. If you come across them at their revels and you carry a moonstone, then they will let you pass unmolested.

Legends that we are all affected by the moon are actually not far wrong. As we are fifty percent water, women's cycles tally with the moon's phases.

Moonstone is good for helping with water retention and infections of the bladder or kidneys.

The Lunantishee

These Faeries are very closely connected to this stone because they themselves as moon Sidhe or moon Faerie suggests. These are the fiercely protective Fae guardians of the blackthorn tree.

Generally these Faeries tend to be antagonistic to humans, but if you carry this stone with you they won't attack.

It is unknown why this state of affairs exists but it's better to carry the stone just in case .

The Lunantishee, like many Faeries and our ancestors before us, worship the moon goddess. Despite there being many mood goddesses found all over the world.

Arianrhod, from Wales, her name means silver wheel, while the Roman goddesses Luna and Diana, whose bow was shaped as a crescent moon.

The Greek Selena, the Aztec Mama Killa, the Finnish Kuu, the list goes on.

Moonstone also helps us get in touch with our feminine intuition and surprisingly it can help us get in touch with our masculine side as well.

Moonstone assists us with new beginnings and fresh starts, helping us cut those ties that bind us to old habits and bad memories.

Rose Quartz

With its beautiful, soft, pink colour, this gentle stone is the stone of love and teaches us not to judge, love is blind, unpredictable, intense, and overwhelming. Love happens when we don't expect it and nearly always catches us off guard.

This beautiful stone helps us balance and see things from others points of view.

Sometimes our love is not reciprocated, and this can cause pain, but no one can force love that is not there.

This stone connects us to unconditional love and helps us appreciate love in all its forms.

It helps us sympathise and empathise with others and helps us become a better person.

This is the stone of the Faerie Queene, her wand is said to be tipped by it so that when it is pointed at you, you know you are loved.

The Gift of Faerie Ancestry

Going back into the ancient past, long before human beings evolved into what we are today, the earth was populated by magical beings.

These beings are what we call today Faeries.

Because these beings have extremely long life's, some still hold the ancestral memory code of our beginnings

They also remember our mistakes and the destructive pattern that we continue to repeat to this day.

They in fact hold the genetic memory of how we began.

They carry not only our mistakes, but of our ancestors' wisdom as well.

Because our food is grown in the soil and the earth itself is controlled by Faerie, then all food that comes from the Earth is Faerie food. Each plant grows directly from Faerie. Every plant, flower and food item has its own diva. Faerie who tends and weaves its energy, pours sunshine and rain into the plants very creation.

All crops grow and fruit ripens because of them.

When our food becomes contaminated by insecticides and it's watered by acid rain or other poisonous chemicals, not only are we poisoned, but also the divas who tend to grow them.

This is no longer Faerie food, therefore each generation onward becomes more disconnected from their lineage and from Fae.

We have become alienated from our own Faerie bloodline.

The Faerie energy which is ours by right is no longer available to us.

This bloodline, called Nwyfre, is denied to us.

Is it any wonder then that more and more of us become isolated and disconnected as to who we really are?

Those of us who suffer the most from this connection are ourselves of Faerie bloodlines.

Many of us, as we research our ancestry will discover that Fae crop up in our lineage time after time.

To research your own Faerie bloodline, start by creating your own Faerie altar. You can use a tray for this if you don't have a lot of room.

This also has the added bonus of being portable, so you can take it outside if you want to.

First, place on your altar a picture of your parents, or grandparents, or something that represents them or the country or city that they came from.

Next, something to represent yourself.

A Hairbrush or comb is ideal.

Now you need something that comes from nature such as a plant, a pine comb, or acorn. Place these on your altar.

Once it's done, you can sit quietly in front of your altar and ask if your ancestors have anything they would like to say to you!

Don't discard anything that comes to you, no matter how crazy it might seem at the time.

This is how I was given my Faerie name.

The word meant nothing to me at the time, but when I googled it, I understood it perfectly.

This is not a one-time ritual by any means, though how far you want to go with it is always your choice.

We have thousands of years of ancestry to remember.

A good idea that I recommend is to repeat it weekly.

Keep a diary and write down everything you discover. Don't discard anything because this could prove to be important later on.

If the information comes through too fast then ask your ancestors for a small break. Remember they might have been waiting for a long time to connect with you, but it's fine to ask them to make an orderly line.

Over the hill and far away,

in a greenwood Faeries play.

They play all night,

and sometimes day.

Over the hill and far away,

there's a stream where Faeries play.

There in the water they play all day.

Over the hill and far away,

there's a bank where I once lay,

but when I woke,

I had to stay,

over the hill and far away.

And now amongst them I must stay,

over the hill and far away.

The Boggart of Finarae

Once upon a Faerie time a long time ago,

or maybe it was just yesterday, a poor farmer rented a cottage in

the village of Finance in the Country of Ireland.

The cottage looked sad and neglected and the farmer's wife had a

kind soft heart, so feeling sorry for the poor little cottage and

because the rent was cheap, they moved in.

It was a small cottage, and the couple had six children, but it did

possess five large cupboards which became warm, cosy places for

the children to sleep.

That night with the children all tucked up cosy, they climbed the

stairs to their own attic bedroom.

Snuggling up with a smile on both their faces, they closed their

eyes.

Neither of them could understand why this charming little cottage

had been left empty for so long.

Crash! The little cottage felt like it was moving.

Bang! The children were awake and screaming.

The farmer went hurrying down those rickety, clickety stairs almost

tumbling in his haste.

But looking around him he saw that nothing was out of place.

Everything was neat and tidy just as his good wife had left it.

But the children were sobbing and told their father that they had seen a short, hairy, little man who had made nasty faces at them.

After scratching his head, the farmer had a good look around him. Checking that the doors and windows were still bolted and barred, he scratched his head again.

Then assuring the children it was just a bad dream that had been caused by all of the excitement of a new home. He settled them back down and went back to bed.

The very next night the same noise occurred

Crash!

Bang!

The little cottage really did shake this time!

Both parents went downstairs this time and found the place neat and tidy as a new pin.

This time though, the children were sobbing even louder, complaining that this time the little man had pinched them.

The next day the farmer went to visit his neighbour and ask him about the cottage.

The neighbour scratched his head and then told our farmer that there was no doubt that what was causing the disturbance, was a Boggart.

Nasty little varmints they are.

The only way to get rid of it is either to have a boxing bout with it, he told him. If you beat the Boggart, it will have to go.

But his neighbour warned him that they don't fight fair.

Well, our farmer, thought, he wasn't as young as he used to be, or as fit.

What is the other option, he asked? He wasn't feeling very optimistic!

You can flit, he was told. But don't let the varmint know about it.

So, the couple set about packing up their things in the quiet and the night they had chosen they left out a wee dram of Whisky for the Boggart, having been assured that this would make him sleep soundly while they made their escape.

That night there was no bang and no crash!

So, with a tear in her eye, because she had come to love the little cottage, they packed up their things, carried their sleeping children out to the cart, and set off.

Just as they were leaving the farmer realised he had left behind his milk churn, so stopped and went back for it. They were all relieved that all remained quiet and oh, so peaceful.

Moving slowly down the country lane, lit only by the moon and stars they encountered their good neighbour coming towards them with his gaggle of geese, heading for the market in the next town.

Raising his hat to the farmer's wife he enquired if they knew yet where they were going.

Before the farmer could reply, a voice from the back of the cart shouted, "We are flitting!" and up jumped the Boggart from the milk churn, a nice warm place he had chosen to sleep on his inebriated night.

So what else could they do but turn back and go home?

And there he still is to today, or at least he might be.

People came from miles around to see him and the farmer and his wife became very rich.

While our Boggart gained lots of fun by throwing stones at his visitors and dancing around the garden naked.

The farmer made a deal with him that now that he was rich he could afford a wee dram to leave out for Boggart.

Boggart agreed and now sleeps all night.

Dryads

Have you ever heard a tree sigh?

Or had a tree branch reach down and brush the top of your head?

If you have, then you have received a blessing from a dryad.

There are thousands of dryads throughout the world, and they have often been described as the lungs of the world.

They are responsible for maintaining the balance of our world.

But today, with deforestation, their job is becoming almost impossible.

Trees have consciousness, they feel pain, in fact, everything in the plant world can feel pain because they have nerves. They hold the elemental wisdom of our planet's survival.

Dryads also hold the energetic space around themselves, with a huge network of roots running for miles underground.

It is through this root system that they can communicate with each other for miles around, it is these roots that anchor these energy fields.

Dryads or Nymphs as the Greeks like to call them, are human in shape and have a particular affinity to the Goddess Artemis, who is known to be a friend to them. They are skilled at wood manipulation and according to legend can create a great oak from an acorn in a day.

They can turn themselves into trees or hide inside trees if they feel under threat.

Dryads and Hamadryads are two types of nature spirits that inhabit trees and thick woodlands.

One famous dryad was Eurydice, the beautiful but ill-fated wife of Orpheus.

According to the legend, Eurydice is killed by a snake while trying to escape the unwelcome advances of Aristaeus. This indicates that dryads are not considered immortal and hamadryads were even more vulnerable as if the tree they inhabited died or was felled, then they also died.

Echo and Narcissus

Echo was a beautiful nymph.

Fond of the woods, she would dance there every day. She was a favourite of Artemis and attended her in the chase.

Echo's big failure was that she loved talking and always had the last word.

One day Hera was seeking her husband who she suspected was amusing himself with the nymphs, Echo knowing this was true sought to detain Hera until the nymphs could make good their escape. When the Goddess realised what Echo was doing she passed sentence on her by saying, "You shall forfeit the use of your tongue with which you sought to deceive me, except for that one purpose you are so fond of, reply. You shall still have the last word, but no power to speak it." Echo caught sight of Narcissus one day at the chase and fell instantly in love with him.

How she longed to speak to him but she was not able to.

One day Narcissus became separated from the hunt, shouting "Whose here?" Echo replied, "I'm here!"

Narcissus looked around, but could see no one, so he called out, "Come!"

Echo replied, "Come!"

On seeing no one, Narcissus cried out "Why do you shout at me?" Poor Echo could only answer with the same.

She hastened to him with all of her heart and tried to throw her arms about him but he recoiled in horror.

"Hands off! I would rather die than be taken by you!"

"Have me!" she repeated, but he left her.

She went to hide her blushes among the woods.

From that time onwards, she lives in caves among the mountains.

But she still responds to anyone who calls her...

The Old Man of the Apple Tree

Without a doubt, this is one of the gentlest Faeries you could ever meet.

Even when the gales blow and the rain falls, while other trees bow their heads away from the elements, our cheerful Apple stands fearless, head high and a smile on its old weather-beaten face.

This applies to only the very old apples.

Over the last twenty years or so many new varieties have arrived, all with their brand new Dryads.

Sadly, this means that the old varieties are dying out and he will go with them.

Please don't let this happen. If you are thinking of planting a tree or even if you were not, if you have the room then please plant one.

You won't regret it for not only do you have an abundance of beautiful apples but this cheery chap as well. Guaranteed to bring a smile to your face.

Legends of the Apple Tree

The fruit of the apple plays many major parts in myths and legends in Celtic mythology.

One such story is of the Irish king Conla, of the fiery hair.

The High King of Connaught fell madly in love with a Faery maiden which once eaten was said to replenish itself becoming whole again.

For an entire month, Cola ate nothing but this apple, and the more he ate it the more he longed for the return of the Faery.

After a month the faerie maiden returned to him in a dream and she invited him in a crystal boat that took them to the other world where he was never seen again.

It was a practice of Celtic spirituality to bury apples with the dead. This was to feed them on their journey to the other world.

The apple is said to contain knowledge and is believed to be the fruit that Eve ate in the garden of Eden.

Though most scholars believe that it was either the Pomegranate or the fig.

In Greek mythology, the Goddess Hera had an apple tree in the centre of her garden that bore golden fruit.

This fruit could give immortality if eaten.

Healing with Apples

Apple's magical healing ability has gone unnoticed and unused in modern days despite the rhyme, 'An apple a day keeps the Doctor away'.

Actually, it really could, or at least go a long way towards it.

Apple in ancient times was called the fruit of the Gods and for good reason.

Warm apple juice with a small sprinkle of cinnamon can ease labour and help the baby and mother relax.

Apple and Clove for toothache.

Regularly eating apples can aid in digestion and help to destroy bad gut bacteria.

In rituals ancient and modern the apple is acknowledged as the fruit of the underworld.

Meaning it is able to sustain us when we venture into those dark places

Such as the realm of death.

Likewise, Druids, Shamans, Magicians, and Witches are protected by the apple as they travel into the other worlds.

Apples and Divination

The blossoms of the apple were sewn into small pouches and given as a love token.

Blackthorn

This tree has strong associations with the faerie realm and it was believed that its roots reached right down into fairyland.

The flowers on this tree are white and grow in great abundance.

Venerated in past times and often avoided probably because of their habit of growing in the strangest of places.

Hawthorn

Hawthorn is above all recognized as the Faeries tree. It can often be found growing alone in fields.

It is considered a portal to the faerie world and is believed by many that if you walk around it three times clockwise, and then three times anti-clockwise, you will actually be able to see the Faerie activity around it.

Rowan

My favourite tree.

All three of these trees have white blossoms, a favourite of the Faeries.

This is a tree of light and fire like Hawthorne.

Sometimes called the wizard tree, or Merlin tree, it gives protection from enchantment, dark magic, and bad luck.

At Samhain, pronounced Sowin people tied two rowan twigs together into the shape of a cross, with a red ribbon to protect them from the spirits of the dead.

It is interesting just how much trees play such a huge part in the Faerie faith and folklore.

Woodlands thrive with myriads of these magical creatures peeping out at us without our knowledge.

It's easy to see how fear of them built up when they were called the hidden people.

The thought of being watched as we skip merrily through the woodland is a definite no-no.

Caves also were a large part of the Celtic faith, dripping water, wells, and streams. I don't think it is a coincidence that all of these secret hiding places that home and hide the Faerie people are all guarded by three elements:

Air.

Earth.

Water

It will come as no surprise to see that the Faeries are themselves created from these very elements and without them, they would cease to be.

Many encounters with Faeries also start with the necessity to protect yourself.

Again coincidence, or is it far more likely that Faeries, like the elements that they are created from, are unstable, changeable, and often unpredictable.

It was almost certainly this unpredictability in our past that earned them the reputation of being evil.

As good and evil are basic Christian tenets, since Faeries are certainly not Christian, then this tag cannot be applied.

Faeries are neither good nor evil, what they are is reactive.

They will react in any given situation. the situation as circumstances dictate and if we want to pursue a tolerable and safe relationship with them then it is up

We learn Faerie etiquette and abide by it.

So evil, no, but capricious, most definitely.

Something else that upsets them are the words 'Thank You'.

Faeries see this as condescending and arrogant.

What they do for us, they do by choice, and no verbal thanks are needed but gratitude is a good alternative.

They love gifts and can be avaricious, anything shiny or that has a musical vibration, such as stones or more crystals, delights them.

They also like sweet food but never ever offer them the flesh of meat or fish.

This is poison to them.

Things like honey, bread (as long as it's not too glutinous), fruit nuts, berries, and even a little piece of cake.

To drink plain water is best for them or as a treat to Elderflower cordial.

In 1880, scholars like W.B. Yeats, who openly studied Faerie law, particularly from the Celtic viewpoint, brought the study of faeries into a certain respectability and was quickly adopted further by the Pre - Raphaelite art movement who illustrated the tales.

Faeries do not eat and digest their food in the same way that we do.

They do not have digestive systems.

They remove the energy from the food and what is left should be buried or fed to birds. Either way, it will be returned back to the Earth.

In the story, 'Soul Cages,' collected by Yeats, Faerie and Folk Tales from Ireland, an otherwise sociable and friendly merrow (a type of merman) collects the souls of drowned sailors.

The merrow places lobster pots at the bottom of the ocean.

The sailors are drawn to them and captured by the merrow and placed on the merrows curiosity shelf.

The Reverend Robert Kirk

Robert Kirk was born in 1644 in Aberfoyle, a country parish near Loch Lomond, Scotland.

He was the seventh son of his parents, James and Mary, an intelligent studious young man who attended the University of St. Andrews and the University of Edinburgh.

After gaining a Bachelor and Master degrees respectively, he then chose to follow his father by becoming a minister in Scotland, the Episcopal.

Despite all of his latent qualities and great mind, what he is remembered for three centuries later, was his belief and the written work he left behind pertaining to Faeries.

He not only believed in them, but regularly went to Aberfoyle hill which was a famous tasting place for them.

For a long time, it was thought that the works he left behind after his untimely death were an amalgamated record of myths and folklore.

Yet, in more recent years, documents came to light that were in fact what he had collected were his own personal journals of his encounters with Faeries.

These new documents claim that Kirk not only wrote about faeries but he visited them regularly on their own land.

Kirk was able to describe in great detail the secrets of both the Seelie and Unseelie courts (friendly and unfriendly faeries).

He was able to describe how they dressed, what they ate, and even their book of light that he claimed to have seen.

He also declared that they called themselves the Faery folk.

Kirk put all of this in a book called:

'The Secret Commonwealth of Elves, Fauns, and Fairies'.

It is said that Kirk often took walks in the evening and invariably gravitated to Aberfoyle hill to communicate with the Fae.

One night he failed to return and a search party discovered his body the next morning on the Faery hill.

Kirk was to all intents and purposes dead.

Yet the day before a family christening he allegedly visited his cousin and told him that he was not in fact dead, but held captive in the underworld.

The Fae being furious at what they saw as his betrayal had put him on trial. Demanding either his life or that as he knew far too much he could never be allowed to return to his own world.

His book was published posthumously by Sir Walter Scott in 1815.

The book is still available to buy, but is hard to read as it is written in the language of the day.

Sidhe on World Upheaval

Many of you will find you are being called healers in the days to come, as the world faces major upheaval as its vibration rises to accommodate the new era approaching.

Some will be called to heal nature areas and the creatures that dwell in it, along with new strains of disease and insect mutations. All indications that you will be going through a tumultuous time.

We here in Faerie have already experienced many of the disasters that you now are about to face and we are willing to guide and help you through this very difficult time.

World governments have buried their heads in the sand for too long.

We in Sidhe, believe that it's time that you, the people, learned the truth.

Covid came like a thief in the night and there have been other diseases that have been hidden from you.

The air we breathed was allowed to be poisoned. The rivers and seas are polluted, and trees and forests have been wilfully cut down.

Insects are being born mutated, while others are dying out.

Each and every living thing upon this earth was created with a purpose in mind. From breaking down the soil and fertilising it to acting as the earth's lungs. The world governments sleepwalk into disaster.

This planet is sick, very sick, and it will be down to the healers to start its recovery.

Next, we need warriors, people who are prepared to challenge big business and government on the way they break promises.

They must stand and demand change. We the Aos Sidhe are here to teach you remote healing.

Some of you will be called to be watchers, this will involve remote scrying, so that you can see what problems the warriors face.

Your world is our world too, and the future of every living thing is dependent upon its survival.

The reason the Sidhe are here amongst us, is to teach remote healing.

This will be done through trance mediumship, allowing both you and your Sidhe soul friend to journey to remote places together to restore the balance of the Earth.

Gunrig explained to me that we must restore the Earth's sacred rhythm otherwise we will be gone anyway.

Healing people will be futile if the earth itself cannot be restored.

The Faery world is also in great danger because they live far closer to the Earth than we do.

Sickness has permeated their world also. Many faces have become dis-eased and disillusioned.

For years they have tended the infrastructure of our natural world by caring for trees, flowers, crops, rivers, and woodland that had already been poisoned.

They themselves are now paying a very high price in not only their physical health, but mental health, and some genetic mutations amongst their young.

Very soon now, contact with Sidhe will quicken up. Many of you will be contacted, some as growers of healing herbs and plants, some of you to travel astrally to places in urgent need of help, and some of you to be gatekeepers. Raising the vibration of the Earth through meditation and prayer.

Some of you will be called to be watchers, these people will journey also to protect the travellers providing help in whatever way is needed. Warriors might be a better way to explain it, by keeping them safe from interference and psychic attack.

Whatever role you are called to, remember that the Fae only uses the sacred circle. It has no start, it has no end. No one part is bigger or smaller than another. The circle is equal just as each and every one of us is.

Healing plants that we should cultivate

Healing with the Faeries starts with Nature, Herbs, and Plants.

This is one of the main goals, and powerful effects of connecting to Faeries.

They can act as a catalyst for profound change; thus we call it "Healing with the Faeries."

"Natural" and "Nature" are two words with the same source. Nutrition and healing, therefore, are intrinsically connected to the ability to speak to Faeries, or at least be open to receiving their wisdom and blessings.

Some of the healing herbs and plants the Faeries instruct us to use are:

Hawthorn.

Turmeric.

Echinacea.

Thyme.

Sage.

Peppermint.

Grape Seed.

Ginger.

Ginkgo.

Flax Seed.

Echinacea.

Tea Tree Oil.

Garlic.

Dandelion.

Lavender.

Cornflower.

Message from Gunrig

To my beloved kith and kin, I bring you heartfelt blessings from my realm to yours.

For too long now we have been separate beings growing more, and more, apart.

Seeking independently the answers to so many questions.

You fail to see that it is only when we are united as one, that the true meaning of existence will start to make sense.

We were meant to be one united people. Not each of our tribe's separate beings searching for unity, yet pulling further and further apart.

We are your soulmates, just as you are ours. Your abilities when mixed with our abilities make us complete.

Now our Earth struggles. Dis-ease damages our beloved Earth mother and when she is harmed, so are we all.

Time is running out and we can no longer tarry.

Can you even begin to imagine a world without plants? Rivers without fish? Trees with blackened leaves, instead of green ones?

Think of the night sky without our sister moon shining in it.

Or a day without brother sun?

Forests that are still and silent without its Faery inhabitants and the creatures who live beside them.

Unthinkable, yes!

Impossible, no, sadly not for that is what awaits us in the very near future unless we act now.

Reach out to us, my cousins, and we will gladly clasp your offered hand. Let us work together and heal our home. We can make a bright and beautiful tomorrow if we unite today.

Placing you in our hopes and blessings for a future of unity and reconciliation.

Gunrig

Faery Offerings

There are many different faces out there and we only know of a very small selection. This is probably because many of them have no desire to have anything to do with us. They don't like us and they certainly don't trust us.

We have the most contact with the face of the summer courts and even they can have an off day.

To please them, and perhaps to get them to trust you, a small offering can work a treat.

Faeries do not have digestive systems so they cannot eat the offering literally but when you see what they leave behind, you will be in no doubt whatsoever that they have accepted it.

They take the energy from it so what is left is very grey in colour. I bury the leftovers.

unsuitable offerings, despite so many people mentioning it is bread, in my experience.

They cannot tolerate gluten very well. Home-made bread or from an artisan baker is ok but sliced bread is not something that I would offer them. The cake is something they do love, but it should only be given occasionally.

I work on the theory that we and they are what we eat.

On holidays, I will either give them a piece of cake or a small piece of chocolate. I will also offer a wee dram of whisky, which they really do enjoy. At other times I give them berries, apple nuts, sometimes a bit of cheese and elderflower cordial.

It is also a good idea to give them their own plate and cup, set it up nicely and leave it for them.

I have a lovely china tea set from my childhood and I use this, but if possible don't use plastic.

Read to them, that is an offering and one that they really appreciate, and it draws them in, and gives them the chance to have a real good look at you.

They will really size you up at this time. They like to smell you so you might feel something landing on your head or brushing your neck.

They will listen to your voice. This is an ideal time for you all to get to know each other

Dance with me,
Wrap your arms around me.
Dance with me,
Under the stars.
Sway with me

While the moon gives her blessing,

Dance with me

I love you so much

Dance with me, don't ever leave

Me.

Dance with me

I long for your touch.

Woman of the Willow

This gentle woodland Faerie is not a Dryad but a Faerie.

Her name suggests that she is associated with sorrow, but this does not mean that she herself is sad.

Far from it, this Faerie will help you come to terms with your loss and her message is that anyone created from matter can never be lost because matter is indestructible.

When your tears won't stop or you are lost in your grief, go and sit under her.

Bower and rest against her. She will shield you from prying eyes.

Once you have met her you can call her to you as she is not confined to the tree.

Her name is Ooonie phonetically O 000 nie.

Which means the giver of comfort.

We lie awake back to back,

you staring at one wall,

me the other.

Like statues, cold and rigid, turned to stone.

I sense you,

feel your silent moan.

What does she want from me?

How much more will she squeeze from

my bones.

We are both tired from the fight.

But convince ourselves that it will be alright.

But we both know that it's over.

So, taking the lead I say, "I understand, I really do.

That you never loved me, the way that I love you".

Your Faerie nature made it so,

so now it's time to let you go.

To sleep in your soft Faerie bower, under a silver moon.

Thousands of eyes upon us,

Yet so alone.

You are smiling in your sleep,

Already lost to me.

I knew this couldn't last!

That someday, somehow, someway, you

would turn to me, "And say "I have to go".

And yes, I know it will end this way,

but one last kiss, I beg you to stay.

I push this thought away.

You are mine for now...

Brownies

I first learned about Brownies from my Welsh Grandmother.

She was a tiny little Welsh woman who raised six sons on her own after her grandfather died very early in life.

She herself was a Faerie Witch and took no nonsense from anybody.

And that included my Father.

They live in human homes and help with the cleaning and other chores and are not averse to babysitting. Many children testify to remembering a tiny Faerie woman reading to them or rocking their cradle.

The absolute worst thing we can do is offer them gifts because they see it as payment and they are not for hire.

However, they do love a bargain, if you were to leave a chocolate biscuit out by mistake or leave a wee dram of the hard stuff, they would consider themselves well served.

One day I was travelling by train to London when I overheard two women sitting directly in front of me talking.

One told her friend that she had a ghost because whenever she went to bed, leaving some washing up till the morning, when she got up it was always done.

As we pulled into the station I apologised for eavesdropping and then told her that ghosts don't do the washing up, what she actually had was a Brownie. I told her a little about them including having to be sneaky to give them something and never giving them clothes. She thanked me and we went our separate ways. Imagine my surprise when arriving for my interview I came face to face with the same woman.

I got the job.

Ballad of a Brownie

When all are asleep and sweet dreams they do keep,

I come out of my home,

like a mouse, I sweep and I brush,

polish and dust.

The windows are starting to glow.

I can bake you fresh bread, wash your pots,

make your bed.

I can simmer and roast with the best,

churn butter, and make cheese.

Bake cakes with great ease, and sing you a song.

Ho, Ho, Ho...

Finding Each Other Again

It seems so long ago since you left me with a kiss.

Then the wind took you away from me.

That is how it seemed to me.

Each day I walk amongst the trees,

searching for the buds and life returning.

Today I saw the first white flower of the snowdrop. I knelt there on

the ground and gently touched it and spoke to it softly.

"Thank you," I whispered.

Because life was returning to the woods and forests.

Soon he would return to me, and we would be,

finding each other again.

The Dreamweavers.

They come dancing each night,

in my dreams

Taking control, weaving their schemes, binding

me with ropes of pearls.

Taking me with them to fly on the wind,

weaving and dancing, we fly through the air.

Tossed by the thermal,

we are tumbled and tossed,

hold on tightly in case I get lost.

They laugh, they jump, they love to play,

seeking fun in every way.

Never fearful, never cowed,

the duck dived through every cloud.

The Thorn Gate

Blackthorn and Hawthorn are the two major trees that the Faerie love the best.

Two druid friends told me of this encounter pretty much as I will tell it to you now.

While out dowsing one day, they noticed two Hawthorn trees standing in a field. They were amazed that they hadn't seen them before, so going over to investigate them more they were even more surprised to discover that mistletoe was growing on both of them, realising that something very special was going on here, they decided to investigate further.

Both trees were identical in height, breadth, and colour.

There was nothing whatsoever to set them apart.

These trees had a story to tell but whether it would tell it remained to be seen. After dowsing around the area and their hazel twigs going off the scale, they decided they would return.

And return they did, every night for a month, and after pouring libations to the trees and numerous offerings, it finally paid dividends for them.

On this particular moonlit night after making generous offerings and a libation, they were given a very clear vision!

They saw sunrise aligning within the gap between both trees on the equinoxes. Then appearing from a mist, the trooping Faeries of the Seelie court emerged. They crossed an almost invisible boundary that shimmered on the ground. After they left the Unseelie court of trooping, Faeries arrived again out of the mist and crossed in the opposite direction.

The courts were quite literally changing over from one realm to the other.

From Spring to Autumn, the Seelie holds court in the summer court, from Autumn to Spring, the Unseelie holds court in the winter court.

We will touch on the court system later.

Conversation with Sidhe

I always know whenever he is around, because not only does the air around me change and shimmer, but I can smell his wondrous fragrance. It smells of pine forest, sunshine and flowers.

Sure enough, there he is, leaning against my kitchen table watching me.

We look at each other and then I ask him how old he is. He bursts out laughing and then tells me that it is no secret, that his world is created on millions and millions of crystals, and that their vibration is so fast that they are in a cocoon if we like, that keeps them in a state of ultimate fitness and optimum health

Then he went on to consider ageing and death to be a product of our low vibration. He points out that our bible speaks of people living into their thousands and women bearing children into their hundreds.

Having read the Bible I know that this is true.

He goes on to say that by eating the flesh of animals who had died in absolute terror and were drenched in adrenalin, we poison ourselves.

He seemed utterly disgusted by this. Faeries never touch the flesh of any meat or foul.

He went on that it was the lack of good husbandry that they objected to more, than actually eating meat. He spoke of animals deserving to live a contented and peaceful life in the fields before they were killed. He explained that far from being dumb animals, are very intelligent. They can sense and smell what is happening to them. They are scared.

I know that this is true because once on a holiday to Greece, I saw a wagon pull up at the hotel with a cabin full of turkeys. Many were already dead on the floor and those that remained were fighting each other and standing on each other's backs in their attempt to hide. This nightmare has never left me. It surfaces day and night to haunt me and the grief goes too deep for tears. My eyes stay dry as my heart breaks. I have never been able to visit Greece since.

He speaks about space travel and tells me that this also plays a part in our climatic change, that irreparable damage has been done to our ozone layer, and asks why?

Pointing out that humans can exist peacefully with ourselves, so why would we want to find even more beings and what would we do to them when we do?

He told me that there were many worlds that exist beside us, and many life forms we know nothing about, and that they would visit us, but first we have to change. We can make a start by acknowledging how little we do know about other worlds.

We can move away from materialism and not feed the greed of so-called big business. They grow fat on our spending and prideful of false success, while so many live-in poverty.

I am beginning to think that they don't think too highly of us where he comes from.

He reads my thoughts and smiles at me, I wouldn't be here if we didn't hold many of you in such high regard. Because of this, we still have hope that we can alter the future and if not then those that will not or cannot see the error of their ways, will be left behind when the great shift comes.

With that, he was gone, and just his fragrance was left behind.

The Wishing Tree

Stay with me a little while because I want to share something with you.

Sit with me beside a Faerie tree that lives its life in a Faerie glen.

A stream scuttles past and I hear it talking to its pebbles.

The grass whispers to the wildflowers and all around us life unfolds, a green beetle hurries past, off to get her shopping.

Walking towards me is my Sidhe friend and with him walks a very beautiful female Sidhe.

My heart contracts with jealousy.

Alright Guys, I am only human, they descend from Gods.

They sit next to me and we sit in silence, just listening to the buzzing of bees and the chattering of insects that live in the long grass.

Everything is peaceful and we start to feel peaceful.

When the female stands up and offers me her hand, I take it and she leads me over to a beautiful rowan tree and tells me to request a twig from it. Not too small and not too big She explains that we are going to make a wand from it but that we must always ask for it. This is called live wood and is so much more powerful than taking what has already been shed on the ground.

No one, she tells me, should ever take without asking. The trees in their root system have nerves and they feel pain just as we do.

Offering me a small very sharp knife, she listens, as I make my request to the tree. After waiting a while, she nods and points to a particle piece connected to a much larger branch. Yet there she instructs me and makes the cut clean and quick.

Afterward, I rested my head against its trunk and thanked it.

The Sidhe seemed very pleased with that.

Then she showed me how to very carefully strip the bark away, gently and carefully she talked to it in her own language.

Then she dipped it in the cool running water and left it to rest on the riverbank in the sun.

Again, we sat in silence, but this time my Sidhe friend smiled at me and reached over and stroked my hand.

I wondered if this made her jealous but her face remained serene and she gave no sign of it.

What seemed much later she retrieves the wand and with her knife carves rune-like marks on it. Then instructs me to do the same on the other side.

She explained that the magic was not in the wand, it was in me. That the wand was simply a more accurate conduit for the energy that the finger as it was prone to be erratic. The energy that cruises down your arm and out through your finger has no conduit, and so is prone to be erratic and unreliable.

A wand is simply a means of directing your energy wherever you point it. But the more you use it, the more power it will retain. It can be used for protection as it can divert bad energy away from you and back to the sender.

But it must never be used in anger or as a means of vengeance. I thanked them and watched them walk away.

Scrying with the Salamanders

I know that central heating is wonderful when you have to get up on a cold morning for work or come home at the end of the day to a warm house. Yes, despite knowing a small part of me still yearns for an open log fire. It reminds of childhoods spent with my Grandparents, of telling stories while we gather close together, roasting chestnuts, though not all memories of the chestnuts are good. I remember well the times they shot out of the fire and burnt my legs.

Grandma used to warm our apple juice up by placing a hot poker into it. And we made toast despite it being smoked, and it still tasted wonderful.

One of my favourite games was looking deep into the fire and asking the salamanders to let us see into Faerieland.

My sisters saw all manner of things such as Dragons and flying boats, but I only ever saw dancing when I looked.

Every time I would see rings of beings dancing and because the flames rose high, and then low, my fingers grew, sometimes tiny that I could barely make them out, and at others, they became so big that I could make out their faces in the flames.

Then quite suddenly I started seeing a male Faerie who would stand in the flames and beckon to me.

At these times Grandma would turn on the lights, an indication that the game was finished, but later she would caution me. The Faeries want you, she would tell me, but promise me that you will never go with them. I gave her my most solemn promise and that satisfied her.

I have never forgotten that promise and it has served me well.

One time they tried to keep me, was the first time that I astral travelled to their kingdom. Suddenly I felt a change in the atmosphere and then I noticed that I was getting furtive glances that made me feel very uneasy. Just as I was thinking that it was time to go, I was approached by a red-haired elf. He was dressed in hooped green leggings and a green tunic.

"Snap," he said, pointing to my hair. "My name is Urick, what's yours?" This felt very off because Fae do not share their names easily, and certainly not with strangers.

"My name is Urick too!" I replied, "What a coincidence. Anyway, I must be leaving now." and began backing toward the door that I had come through, but not before I saw a flash of anger in his eyes. He took hold of my hand and tried to pull me back into the banquet hall!

All the time he was doing this he kept nervously looking behind him. "Your name is not really Urick?" he asked me.

"No, I replied, then neither is yours, so it will serve for tonight."

His grip tightened and I knew he was very angry at being found out. It's really not a very good idea to upset the Fae anywhere but in their own home is a definite no-no.

The only thing that I could think of was to call my animal totem and almost instantly he was there standing in the doorway. Ulrick or whoever it was, dropped my hand and instantly backed away.

So, who is my animal totem then? a bear? a wolf? a panther?

No, none of these things.

My animal totem is a turtle, the oldest creature on earth. He holds up the world and carries all the wisdom of creation on his back.

Fire

We are dancing in the fire,

Red, gold, and orange.

As we dance within the fire,

the heat is rising.

As you hold me in your arms,

desire grows.

Kiss me in the fire.

I feel no danger when

you kiss me in the fire.

All fear goes.

Touch me in the fire.

My body yearns for you to touch

me in the fire,

My passion grows.

Now I'm consumed within the fire.

The flames rise higher.

I'm devoured within the fire,

no turning back now!

I become one within the fire

And I'm consumed.

Element Bath Oil

Earth Element.

Using a sterilised glass bottle, and following this charm exactly:

2 drops of rosewood essential oil.

2 drops of Cedarwood.

2 drops of Jupiter.

2 drops of Geranium.

100 mls of sweet almond oil.

Place the almond oil in the bottle, then using a dropper, add the oils one at a time.

Place the lid on and shake really well.

Always shake well before use.

This blend is very good for grounding yourself before a ritual or when meeting people who drain you. You can dab it on your wrists or behind the knees, but I wouldn't use it on my neck if it's exposed to direct sunlight.

Fire element, because its primary element is transformation, in its alchemical tradition, the fire element is considered the most important of all of the elements.

Being both creative and destructive, always in motion and fluidity, ever-changing.

It signifies rebirth and banishes the old making way for the new.

Follow as for earth:

2 drops of Frankincense oil

4 drops of cinnamon oil

2 drops of Clary sage

Air Element

Follow exactly the same

3 drops of Rose

2 drops of Clary sage

2 drops of orange oil.

Water Element

3 drops of Bergamot.

3 drops of Chamomile.

3 drops of lemon.

If kept in a cool dark place they should keep for three months.

Stories and songs have always contained alchemy. They contain magic so strong that they can make us believe lies and lose ourselves in make-believe lands.

Bards were often Druids who knew the old stories and rhymes. They were welcomed wherever they went and were fed and given a bed for entertainment, but sometimes they had a hidden agenda. Because they had access to everywhere, they could often be sent as spies to deliberately spread falsehoods.

Beware you!
The teller of tales,
for into the twilight of Earth, Fire, and Water,
of enduring hearts,
and fair fierce women.
The queen and the fool.
The lost and unwary,
held fast in the web of the friends of the Faerie
A visionary awaits,
Called on by village ghosts, while
a voice calls from enchanted woods,
for mortal help.
The coward closes his ears and feigns sleep,
torn between belief and unbelief.

While the old town lies sleeping,

windows sightless in the dark.

People dream dreams that have no morals.

By the roadside, the lady of the hills stands waiting.

Beware then the teller of tales.

Who can weave in his sonnets and stories of old?

Of fiddlers paid for their music in gold,

while Witches and Goblins by moonlight grow bold.

Faeries are part of nature, a fundamental part, so it stands to reason that they can be found in nature, for the simple reason they can't be taken out of it.

Therefore, you see and interact with them on a daily basis, whether you have a garden or not.

All you have to do, to interact with them more fully, is to go through the seven Faerie doors and I am going to help you do that. You won't see them if you don't look and that is a big part of the problem.

The first Faerie door is **Perception**.

When you leave the house each morning, give yourself an extra five minutes to really look at the first tree that you see. Look at the shape of the leaves, can you recognize what kind of tree it is?

Look at how it moves if there is a wind about. Look at its trunk, can you see a face in it?

Are you able to touch it, if not, then try and imagine how the leaves would feel?

Close your eyes and see it in your mind's eye, then open them again, was your vision accurate?

And if it was well done you have passed through your first Faerie door.

If it wasn't, then why wasn't it?

Try again the next day. No prizes for being first, so keep going.

Door Two

The second faerie door is **Acknowledgment.**

I believe "That every time a child says, I don't believe in faeries,

A Faerie dies."

J M Barrie

Peter Pan 1860-1937

Acknowledge that you believe in them.

I am not asking you to take out a full-page spread in your local paper, of course not.

But simply in your natural spaces say hello good people, how are you today, may the mother bless you.

That's not hard to do and soon you will see rewards.

Do this and you will walk through the second Faerie door.

Door Three

The third Faerie door is **Listening**.

We are all created on a single note, one perfect note that joins us to the spheres, this note is not only for this life, it follows us through every life.

Each time we are born we will change our appearance, but our note stays the same. That is how we recognize each other. Have you ever wondered how you can like someone instantly or take an instant dislike to somebody?

Well now you know, you recognise their note.

Anyway, back to the business in hand, plants sing, trees sing, shrubs sing, and flowers sing. You must learn to listen.

I recommend you buy a new plant and then sit with it in light meditation.

When you can do this, you can pass through door three.

Door 4

The forth door is **Seeing.**

Believe it or not, seeing your first Faerie could be a disappointment at least if you are expecting Tinkerbell. Often your first sighting will be no more than a flash of light. This shouldn't surprise you though because they are created from light.

You might even realise that you have been seeing them all of your life. This is not to say that they cannot take on form because they can and often do. But only after you have formed a relationship with them.

Once you can do this you can pass through the fourth door.

Door Five

Door five is **Being.**

I am, therefore I exist, connected with your own divinity. Acknowledge your right to be here.

You are as good as anybody, you have the same rights as anybody and if you want to see their face, or interact with them, then it is up to them and nobody else.

This is about claiming your own place in the great cosmic scheme of things. You were not born to be a bystander, you were born to take your place, a place that was ordained for you from the very start of creation.

Don't apologise to anyone for being here, you belong here.

When you are ready to do this, you can go through door five.

Door Six

Door six is **Knowing**.

To simply know, means that you are connected to the cosmic life force.

To see is not always to believe, hearing is often the same, but knowing is very different. The hard part is accepting that you know. We learn through many different experiences, and unfortunately, we learn most from the hurtful ones.

These are the life lessons that stay with us the longest.

When you attain this point, that you have confidence in knowing, and trust yourself, then you can pass through door six.

Door Seven

Door seven is **Sharing**.

Now that you have travelled along the crooked path to Faerie and confidently gone unhindered through six doorways, it is time to work in partnership with them.

They are now very aware of you, even if they weren't before.

You have piqued their interest and faeries are extremely curious.

By now they are probably sitting on your window ledge looking in at you or sitting on the bonnet of your car to see where you are going.

Now you are no longer doing this on your own.

They are as eager to communicate as you are.

You will now be able to sense a change in atmosphere or energy. You will recognise when they are about and you can start leaving offerings. If you have not done this before then they like a bowl that is only used for them.

Not plastic, and an egg cup will do for liquid. Freshwater or elderflower cordial is what I use.

Faeries are very polite, they need time to look you over and make their minds up.

Don't take it badly if they suddenly pull back from you?

It simply means they decided you're not quite compatible. We can't get on with everybody, and neither can they. If your offering is accepted then they have said yes, if not, there are plenty more out there that will suit you just fine. As a general rule, you should leave an offering for at least three days. Remember it's theirs now, you gave it to them.

After three days bury what's left for the creatures of the soil.

Names

Much is said about not giving them your name, because names have power.

While that is certainly true and they won't give you their name until they are absolutely sure of you, and that can take years.

You can be very certain that they already know yours.

These guys are not stupid. They have been watching you for weeks now.

They have heard your family use your name numerous times by now.

They have heard neighbours and friends use it. Delivery men use it. In fact, they have probably been sitting on the postman's shoulders. But they are polite and usually don't use it until you give them permission.

So don't give it, until they allow you to know theirs.

You can ask to be known by a nickname, and ask them what you should call them.

Faeries and Sexuality

Faeries are very sexual beings and they do have a strong sexual appetite.

After all, these beings make no bones about living for pleasure. They also like variation and are bi-sexual.

Both male and female Faeries do mate with humans, by this I am talking about the higher Fae who closely resemble ourselves.

They have always been fascinated by us and can be jealous of our physicality. The one thing we have that they don't is our ability to touch, taste, and feel. Because they themselves are non-physical, then they cannot feel on our physical level. What they can do is experience sensation through the intellect.

I have never experienced tantric sex, but I have experienced a very high charged coupling with a Sidhe.

They quite happily mate with both males and females and are good breeders. Any child born from such a union will be extremely beautiful, they will be gifted in music and art.

Although the Fae make wonderful lovers, they will never make faithful lovers. They have no understanding at all of fidelity. In their world they live in the moment and when they want something they see no reason not to have us. They also don't understand jealousy, and under no circumstances would they tolerate a relationship where they were subjected to it.

Much has been said about Changelings, and one explanation for them taking babies as if they were their own. The mother almost always raises a half-faerie child in her own world, but should they feel the child is being neglected or cruelly treated, then they will take it

Faerie women can form deep sexual relationships with human women and the same applies to men, faerie sexuality is very fluid and changeable.

If a half-faerie child is taken away to faerie then they will, in time, become fully faerie. This is achieved by its vibration increasing in tune with the dimension they are now living in. The vibration of crystals is what causes this elevation and young children can adapt to it far more easily than an adult can.

In cases where adults are located in faeries, many are unable to adjust to the changes and die. Sometimes they live for a few years. This is the reason many people return after seven years because this seems to be the period when they start to deteriorate.

Some Fae move to live here amongst us, but usually if a Fae is to live as one of us for a particular reason, they are usually born here. I came across this poem recently and thought of sharing it. It is out of copyright and sadly the author is unknown. But we clearly have studs among our own men.

Full night,

seven times by her he lay.

She said "Man you like your play?

What woman, in her bower,

can deal with thee?

I pray you, Thomas, leave me be."

Anon.

Sidhe on Anger

I asked my Sidhe friend how we could make our own start on helping our planet. What follows is his reply:

It is not that Sidhe don't get angry, we do, but we have learned through experience to temper our response to it.

The planet becomes seriously ill not only through the poisons, but also comes from greedy manufacturers or the government playing God.

Think carefully about how much damage anger can cause?

This is part of the fire element after all, and the elements were equally divided at creation. But anger increases the power of this element and increases it over the others. Anger first and foremost, is a physical reaction that is caused often by a nonphysical stimulus. Something angers you, mentally then the heat rises in you physically, very quickly followed by its expulsion. You allow that anger to escape out into the atmosphere.

Now it starts to rise (air) becomes involved, and carries it high into the atmosphere where it spreads across the Earth as a poison that increases density and toxicity.

Still not done, it falls then as rain soaks deep into the earth. We now have all of the elements out of their natural control. Which creates instability.

"Do you understand me? " he asks. I nod my head.

In order to reduce the destructive forces harming our planet, each and every one of us has to take a deeply, honest look at ourselves, and we realise that this is not easy. We struggled also, but we eventually were able to overcome our ego and confront our failings. This is probably one of the biggest challenges we all must make.

Address the stimuli that make you angry, then search your heart for a better way of dealing with it.

You cannot change the stimuli, it's true, but you can change how you react to them!

Every part of your being was designed to react in ways that create the reality of what you most desire. Change your desire into understanding how best to change your perception and your reaction to things.

Try affirmations several times a day, what you say, creates who you are. If you say, for example, that you wish to remove anger from yourself and replace it with calm and understanding and if you say it often enough, it will become your reality.

Words bring things into creation. To change what is being created simply change your words.

Consider then how your perception of things can affect the reality of others around you. Not only in your locality but all over the world.

Low mood can lead to mental illness, which can lead to feelings of isolation, that in turn can lead to thoughts of suicide, and these feelings can manifest in people thousands of miles away.

He looks at me thoughtfully and asks me again if I understand his words, again I nod my head.

How can I change should be the question on everyone's lips? How can I save the earth? The answer is to change yourself first, and the rest will follow.

Then he is gone.

This is an accurate channeling from Gunrig, my Sidhe guide.

Pendulums

A good way to find out if you have Fae in your garden or house is by using a pendulum. Many are available in shops and online. I recommend that you touch it first. Hold it in your hand in a closed fist, not too tight, but tight enough to be able to feel its response to you. If you get a good strong pulsation to your heartbeat, then you have found the one for you.

They don't have to cost the earth, and bigger is not always better, the important thing is that it is right for you.

I bought my present one in a wonderful little shop in Portpatrick on the isle of Skye.

I walked past it at first, then halfway down the street I turned around and went back.

It is only small on a silver chain but it almost jumped off the stand at me.

Even the assistant laughed and said, "It wants to go home with you." So, it did!

First, you have to calibrate it and see which way is 'yes' and which way is 'no'.

Ask a question such as "Is my dog called fluffy?"

There is no point in asking it something you don't know the answer to.

The way it swings will be your reply.

Try this as many times as you want to, until you feel comfortable.

Then walk around your home.

Kitchens, and bathrooms are good places for Water Fae, gardens for nature Fae, and the rest of the house for others.

They can come down chimneys, and windows and doors, because they can come through them.

You will need to wash it in spring water after each use and re-calibrate it each time you use it.

But do use caution! Test it well.

There was a time when I suspected my partner was having an affair with my best friend.

Their behaviour was off somehow.

When together, they barely acknowledged each other, and while he would make a great fuss of me, sitting with his arms around me and such, she could barely look me in the eye.

So, confiding in my sister I arranged a dinner party, with just the four of us. My sister was there as the observer. Afterwards, she agreed that something was going on.

So, I turned to my pendulum.

"Is --- having an affair?" I asked.

It swung into action almost spinning out of orbit. Thank you, I responded in order to stop it.

"Is it with ---? I asked"

Again, I got the same response.

I was far more heartbroken over her because we had been friends since school.

I had an enormous showdown with her and she broke down in tears. Then she told me that she had seen him with another woman we both knew at school. She shared the same Christian name as my best friend.

It seems she had told him to either tell me or she would.

Her cold behaviour with him was because of this and she felt bad because she had not come straight round to tell me.

So, like I said, caution!

Merfolk

One time I was on a short holiday with three friends. We were a very close-knit group and shared the same interests (Faeries).

This cottage was on Holy Island connected to the mainland of the UK by a causeway.

We loved going here because once the ride came in you were completely cut off unless you went by boat.

This island has a millennium of history. Invaded and occupied by the Vikings in the 8th century, reclaimed by Christians and then invaded again by pagans. Here the pendulum still swings backward and forwards. It is without a very holy island, but it is not Christianity that holds sway here.

Arriving at a lovely little clifftop cottage all four of us came to a stop at the front door. Each waiting for the other to go first. I led the way, while the atmosphere was not exactly hostile it was watchful. We could all feel our chests starting to feel tight.

On closer inspection, we found the owner's belongings still there, including toiletries in the bathroom cabinet, and clothes in the wardrobe.

The walls were painted blue in every room with huge murals of fish all over them. There was a bedroom none of us wanted to sleep in, so we doubled up.

The lounge had a beautiful hand-carved fireplace, it must have been at least eight feet in height, and five in breadth.

Down the full length of one side was a merman. His tail started at the top and his webbed fingers rested at the bottom.

On the other side was an exact replica, only this was female. The carvings were stunning in their workmanship, but the figures were horrific. Their faces were hideous, but also deeply mesmerising. It was hard to look away.

Their faces were elongated like a cod, ending in a point. They came straight out instead of down like ours. Their eyes were round and protruding, and were without eyelashes.

None of us said anything, we were all stunned! We all agreed though that this place had a guardian and an extremely powerful one.

We saw our stay out, but we were on our very best behaviour.

Whoever had carved these images had without doubt seen them. They were not the creation of somebody's imagination.

So, we cleaned up daily. Washed our pots after we used them and make our beds each morning.

We would stand and watch the ocean from the clifftop and not one of us had any doubts that these mere creatures were out there.

Autumn is dying and as the cold winds sweep across the land.

Winter has arrived. The trees have lost their leaves and the birds their homes seeking warmth and protection from the cruel snows and frosts that they know are on their way. Temperatures drop dramatically.

Tiny creatures and insects burrow deep in crevices and holes to wait out the winter. For those that did not store up food for the winter the time is perilous!

The frozen lands of winter are perilous for those who are unprepared.

Life is harsh, and darkness dominates these cold hostile lands.

Mortals leave offerings to the winter Fae in the hope of being protected and spared the harshest price of winter. Others bar their doors with nails in the hope that the Fae will not pay a visit to them. They seek out their food in the hope that they can make it last.

Any deals made with the winter Fae carry a more than usual amount of risk. Winter is a time of death and loss, fear from the winter court holds sway over the dark cold months. They become empowered by the desolation around them and make the most of the fear and uncertainty that pervades the air.

Powerful Ice hags roam the night, knocking on locked doors and pleading to be allowed in by the fire. Occupants huddle together for comfort, they chant ancient charms and spells of protection that might or might not send her on her way, to menace someone else.

Out of the raging blizzards come distorted shapes, monstrous, unidentifiable, barely visible, as they loom out of the darkness. Foul creatures that rejoice in the dark, eat up fear and rejoice in sorrow, death, and loss. The wise keep their doors barred and say their prayers to their gods for protection. The foolish let them in.

The Unseelie Fae

When icicles hang by the wall,
and Dick, the shepherd, blows his nail.
And Tom bears logs into the hall,
and milk comes frozen from the pail.
When blood is nipped, and ways are foul,
then nightly sings the staring owl,
To-whoo
To-Whit, To-Woo, a merry note,
While greasy Joan stirs the pot.

When all aloud the wind doth blow,
and coughing drowns the parson's saw,
and birds sit brooding in the snow,
and Marian's nose looks red and raw.
When roasted crabs hiss in the bowl,

then nightly sings the staring Owl,

To- whit, to-whoo, a merry note,

While greasy Joan doth stir the pot.

William Shakespeare, Love Labours lost.

Faerie protection dates back thousands of years and can consist of various forms used to drive off dark Fae while being welcoming to the kinder, more helpful faeries.

One of the best forms of protection against the dark Fae taking up residence in your home is to invite your ancestors and Gods into your home. Once they take up residence they will provide protection from any dark Fae. We all know about Iron but windchimes and the ringing of bells are also very effective in keeping unwanted things far away. Put chimes or bells on your gate post and hang them from the ceiling just inside your door or window. Turn an item of clothing inside out and it will protect you from being Pixi-led. Being Pixi-led might sound like fun, but believe me it is not. After covering the same ground over and over again sometimes for many hours not only do you think that you are going insane, but you genuinely fear never getting out and dying there!

Faerie light-some people like to use this method during meditation. Known as the circle of light it consists of visualisation techniques.

First, relax and let your mind calm and empty, imagine a blank screen in front of you. Now see your home in all its detail on this screen, once you have done this imagine looking into the window and seeing your home in colour, your family, friends and yourself, pets, and belongings that you treasure. Once you have done this visualise a deep golden light descending on your home and everything you have placed in it. Throw a brick at the window and see it bounce off. This protection is invincible, nothing can penetrate it. Another smaller one for when you go out alone is to visualise a golden egg that fits your body perfectly. If you feel threatened then simply step into your golden egg, run your hands around it feeling for any tears or splits, and gently smooth it out. Now step inside it. This is your shield of protection. It is the one I myself use particularly when I am working alone.

The Unseelie Fae of the winter court is often called the unholy court but to be honest, they are no more unholy than the Seelie court. They are both capricious, changeable, and reactive. Is a bear evil because it kills to survive? To be evil surely is to go against what nature intended, to know and understand the ramifications of your actions is wicked but doing it anyway. Fae do not do this, they certainly don't think ahead to the outcome of their behaviour. They are part of nature, and nature can give us a beautiful sunny day or it can give us a hurricane.

The Unseelie then are more likely to harm us than help us and no offence is necessary to turn them against us, unlike the Seelie who will be friendly unless we offend them.

Faerie can be helpful or not helpful, it's true that you can expect less help and even a hindrance from the Unseelie court. But don't be lulled into thinking that the Seelie Fae are angels because they certainly aren't. The fate of this court do breed between themselves and so the genetic mutations that are here, do account for some of the nightmarish tales that have come down to us from legend and folklore. So, who makes up the hierarchy of the winter court and how is it structured?

MAB

Heads the court of winter with her consort, King Fin. She also has a lover, Prince Frost who tore out his heart to give to her to prove his devotion.

When Shakespeare portrayed her in his play Romeo and Juliet she was already well known in the Faerie lore of Great Britain.

Romeo's friend Mercurio speaks of her thus:

O, then, I see Queen Mab hath been with you.

She is the Faeries 'midwife', and she comes

in shape no bigger than an agate-stone

on the fore-finger of an alderman.

Drawn with a team of little atomies,

Athwart men's noses as they lie asleep.

Her wagon -spokes made of long spinner legs.

The cover of the wings of grasshoppers,

the traces of the smallest spider's web,

the collars of the moonshine's watery beams,

her whip of cricket's bone, the lash of film,

her wagoner a small grey-coated gnat,

Not so big as a round little worm,

Pric'd from the lazy finger of a maid.

Her chariot is an empty hazel-nut.

Shakespeare's Romeo and Juliet.

So, we know that Mab is a tiny Faerie that rides around in a hazel nutshell. But let us remember then that how they appear to us is extremely selective. They appear any way that suits them at any given moment and alter their appearance at will.

Whatever her size Mab is possibly the oldest Faerie Queene of all and was known long before Shakespeare wrote his plays.

Some associate her with Maeve

Maeve, Maev, Maiv, is both a Celtic Goddess and a Faerie Queene, she holds a powerful place in Celtic mythology. Her beauty and sexual prowess were legendary. No High King could be crowned without first having the ceremony consummate in her bed.

Her husband, Eochaid, was only allowed to marry her because he was a man completely without jealousy.

The marriage was not a good one and Maeve eventually left him.

Legend tells her that she murdered her own sister while she was pregnant by drowning her. By some miracle, the child survived.

The child, a boy called Furbaide, later a man, killed Maeve in revenge for his mother's death.

Maeve is said to be buried in a forty-foot high stone cairn, standing upright and facing her enemies in the North.

Even in modern times, her legend lives on and she is venerated as the symbol of the power of women over men in terms of cunning, sexuality, and power.

Shelley wrote of her:

Behold the chariot of the Faerie Queen!

Celestial courses paw the unyielding air,

their filmy pennons at her word unfurl,

and stop obedient to the reins of light.

These the Queen of Spells drew in.

She spread a charm around the spot,

And, leaning gracefully from the ethereal car,

long did she gaze, and silently

upon the slumbering maid.

Queene Mab

Percy Bysshe Shelley

Dedicated to his wife, Harriet. 1813

The Ice Maid

This role is taken by a young female Faerie, and she reigns for a year. Part of her job is to wait on the winter Queen and report to her if any of the courts have been in breach of protocol or Fae law. This is a very beautiful Faerie who will be dressed in frost, itself being painted onto her skin, in patterns of white and silver.

She wears a crown of small crystal gems and her small tender feet are painted in swirls of frost.

Any mortal man who saw her would instantly fall head over heels in love with her and forget all former obligations.

If they make love with her, however, they will freeze to death. It is a measure of her seductive powers though that even knowing this many still choose to forfeit their life for one kiss from this Faerie maid.

She is gifted with music and it is said her voice can beguile all who hear it.

The Ice Mother

This Faery is very often the same Faery who was the frost maiden the previous year.

In this persona, she must age and take on the role of mother to the entire court.

In this role we see her reach maturity as she goes from girl to woman.

She also represents the winter as it goes from its first early snows and blizzards to a more settled cold that no longer takes us by surprise.

This is a more mellow time, a time for reflection and telling stories around a blazing fire. A time to light the lamps and draw together in the firelight and give thanks for all that you have.

The Snow Crone

Now she grows fully into her wisdom and power, with the beauty of her age and wisdom she has no equal. Second in power only to Queen Mab herself.

A direct manifestation of the Goddess herself

In modern society where youth and physical beauty is worshipped, we neglect the crone to our cost.

In her, we see the promise of renewal as one life draws its conclusion. We can look back at all that we have achieved and give gratitude for a life well-lived.

We also have the promise of a new spring, new life, and new chances to start again.

The North Wind

Brings snow, so we are told, in the nursery rhyme, that this winter spirit is extremely powerful and no one should ever call it without very good reason.

Winter cannot arrive before this spirit has announced herself and when she does arrive, she will carry hundreds of Fae riding on her back. Only then can the winter court convene.

After the arrival of the north wind, it becomes a free for all, as fate arrives in their thousands.

Chione

This very beautiful frost princess is said to rival Mab in beauty, and Mab has been jealous on more than one occasion. She is believed to be Mab's daughter, by the Prince of frost,
Although her beauty is great her character isn't as she is reported to be vain and shallow.

The Frost Prince

Lover to Mab and father to Chione, the prince of frost is indolent. He lives the life of a courtier at the winter court.
Legend tells us that he is the son of Titania and Oberon who rule the summer court. He was shunned and even hated by another Fae at the Summer court.
The fate of winter however united under him. He was becoming so powerful that Mab made him her consort lover to keep her eye on both him and his ambition.
Once upon a time, the Prince of Frost was known as the Sun Prince and he ruled his realm with love and kindness.

Among his people were three sisters called the Daughters of Delight. The most beautiful of them was called Sharara.

She and her prince were deeply in love until she became bored with the life they were living of endless revelry, so she decided to visit the mortal reign for a change. Here she fell deeply in love with a mortal man.

When the Sun Prince discovered this, he was very jealous and ordered her to return and honour her promise to him.

Being too scared to face him, and afraid of what he would do to her mortal lover she made a bargain with the Raven Queen that cast her soul and the soul of her lover forward in time. Hoping that this would give the prince time to cool down and heal.

Instead, the prince grew more and more bitter with sorrow until one day the sun never shone and his kingdom was cast into gloom. He left his kingdom, but his heart had turned to ice.

Other members of the Winter court:

Kelpie is a Scottish water horse that lives in deep rivers and lochs. He entices weary travellers to climb up onto his back then rides into the waters and drowns them before devouring them.

Bean Sidhe, is a beautiful Faerie woman, who can be heard keening and wailing outside the home of someone soon to die.

Red Caps. These faeries get their name, as you would surmise because of their red caps, which are soaked in their victim's blood and must never dry out, or they will lose their magic.

Kelpie is also a water horse that drowns and eats their victims.

Barghest. Native to the Northern part of England, this is a monstrous black dog with sharp teeth and claws. They have also been known to eat their victims.

Boggart is small and hairy and lives in bogs and wetlands but some have been known to live in houses where the mistress is slovenly. More of a nuisance than anything else, but they can drive you to distraction.

Bean Night

A Scottish female spirit who is the harbinger of death. Centuries ago she was a beautiful young woman with blood-red lips. She was the daughter of a wealthy landowner who fell in love with a peasant.

Her father on the other hand, forbade the marriage and instead promised her to an old man instead. Heartbroken, she took her own life.

Crying over her grave, her young lover wept over her grave and pleaded for her to return. One year, later on the anniversary, she did return.

Going first to her father while he slept, she placed her mouth over his and sucked his life from him. Then she went to the old man who had been her husband and treated her cruelly, here she bit him and drank his blood.

Now on her anniversary, she returns again to feed on the blood of the unwary.

Pooka

Of all the supernatural beings that are said to populate Ireland, none are more feared than the Pooka. This is a shape-shifting Goblin, so you might not even know that you have encountered one until it is too late.

His name is believed to have derived from a Scandinavian spirit called Pook, or Puka, which means nature spirit.

This mischievous spirit is said to come out after dark and steal children away.

Magic of The Winter Fae

This has its root in chaos magic and they often favour spells of the storm and cold elemental magic along with illusionary and nature magic.

There are things in this court that not even the most powerful of Fae would dare to dabble in because it is home to dreams but nightmares as well.

This is nebulous and not really understood, existing on the very fringes of Faerie are creatures of such darkness and gloom that nobody dares speak their name. While they do exist on the fringe of Faerie, they are not really a part of the Fae.

Shadow magic, is not really magic at all in its purest form, because this kind of magic requires a sacrifice of a part of oneself to the shadow in exchange for the ability to shape it or to gain from the dark benefits it offers.

There is far more to the Faerie realm than most of us realise, while I still maintain that they are not evil as we know it, they certainly can become dangerous and mischievous as those of you who have contact with them will be well aware of.

Their energies can be very stimulating and create altered states of consciousness.

For example, Pixies are often accused of leading people around in circles or Pixie led, they may do this to some, but in other instances coming into contact with their energy, which is very strong, can in fact alter your consciousness to such a degree that you yourself don't truly know where you are going.

The pixies bless them and are left sitting up in the trees watching this carry on in total perplexity.

Looking at us, rather than looking at each other, and saying, "These humans are strange creatures!" No wonder they laugh and find it funny.

Those of the Fae realm respond to life with such feelings and they have a far greater understanding of universal energies. This is partly because they are unhampered by a physical body as we are.

The higher Fae, such as Sidhe and Elves, often show themselves in human form and can when they want to pass themselves off as human. These higher Fae do have a sense of ethics, and only a few renegades would be found in the winter court. In general, they belong to the summer court.

Never assume you know the Fae, even if you have been working with them for a long period. You don't know them and you never will. Yes, they can be wonderful but the very same Fae can be deadly.

I wanted to write this book because there is so much bad information going around right now, and much of it is downright dangerous. These beings have more power in their little finger than we could ever begin to imagine. And even the Seelie Fae, the ones we can make friendships with, having to be treated with the utmost respect.

It works two ways, and they will treat you with the same respect and kindness. If they have no reason to harm you, then they won't, but the Unseelie will, they don't need a reason. Remember that if you choose to deal with them.

I have heard stories of people who unknowingly have littered a Faerie hill or bush, or even a pathway and the Fae have responded with devastating consequences. If you are out in nature, then pick up your litter. It is not only the right thing to do, but it's also much safer.

Treat them always as valued guests, value them just as much. If they refuse to help you, accept it.

They don't owe us anything, remember that.

The truth is that they will not tiptoe around your feelings, they can't dissemble.

Truth is the raw essence of the nature of things, unchanged, unfiltered.

Truth is not just words, it's also actions and self. Truth is always at the heart of nature. Faeries don't only speak the truth, their version of it at least, they are true and when we are dealing with them, we must be also.

Is a shark evil because it kills, no of course not, it is only being true to its nature, it is simply reactive, it needs food it will take it. It does not consider the consequences of its actions because it does not understand them, neither do Fae .

They don't think as we do, they don't feel as we do, and they certainly don't experience grief or loss.

So while accepting that they certainly can be dangerous and some more than others, but because they can't understand the consequences of their actions, they can't be evil.

Faerie Magic

Faeries are very proficient at magic, particularly enchantment, in this they can alter a person's state of consciousness.

Using magic and spells, they are able to manipulate a situation and turn it to their own advantage. While under this spell, a person will lose all sense of free will and will be in a state of high excitement, even ecstasy, while doing something they would not normally do. In a Midsummer Night's Dream, Titania falls in love with a Donkey, while Helena asks a boy to treat her like a dog.

Enchantment then is to beguile, to change our reality into something that amuses Faerie.

Elemental Magic

This magic refers to the magic that uses any or all of the elements. Earth, Air, Fire, and Water. Energy and intent are the very foundation of this kind of magic allowing the spell caster to use the weather for their own purpose. This includes calling in the Elemental spirits such as Gnomes Earth, Undies Water, Sylphs Air, and Salamanders.

This is a dynamic practice because it does deal with nature and nature, which as we know can be very capricious.

Consider how a fire warms and helps keep us alive, or how it can burn and destroy, or rain that nourishes plants, but as a tsunami, destroys. Those who seek to work with elemental magic need to study it well and be sure that they can control it.

This discipline of magic needs the user to understand that the elements are neutral by nature. These elements can be used for great good such as creating rain during a drought, but they can also be used for great evil also they can get out of control if someone not adequately trained loses control of them.

Manipulation

The effects of faerie influence are very real and very strong, the Fae enjoys manipulating humans and playing games with our reality, they are very good at it.

They can affect our emotions by either making us euphoric and blissful or taking us down into the pits of despair. This is one reason why we find them so hard to resist, whenever they seek to lure someone into their vast web their lure can be hypnotic. They know exactly how to play on your emotions and your feelings.

This should always serve as a warning and an eye-opener, people do not go screaming and fighting into the web of faerie, they go dancing.

Fae is addictive, and there is something in our makeup that draws us irresistibly to them.

Once a Fae has touched you, whether you were aware of it or not, you will never be entirely free from them.

So what happens if a Fae does take you away with them? In my research, it became obvious that no one ever comes back in the same way that they went. Despite the cloak that has been spread over the subject, it is a fact that mental hospitals and asylums were full of people that came back unable to cope or settle back in their homes.

And eventually have been taken away and considered mad or insane.

Others have been physically changed, there are many cases on record of people who thought that they dance all night in a Faery ring, only to discover with the dawn, that they have danced for weeks and are nothing more than skin and bone.

Some refuse to eat and drink after tasting Faery food.

They reject everything that's offered to them eventually dying from starvation. Others have had faerie lovers and even faerie children and they grieve for them. Still, others age instantly and go from being young and vibrant to old the instant they return.

Some of the winter courts can be terrifying. Others might want you with them because you are gifting in music or singing. The reason they took you is numerous. Some might seek to sell you as a servant, or sex slave!

Others might turn you into something beautiful for their gardens, half-tree and half-human, and I can feel you recoil now, just as I did when I learned of this part of Faerie, will eat you. Not with a knife and fork, obviously, but they will drink your blood and drain your essence. Others will keep you because they like you and make you part of their family. The reasons are many and whatever happens, you will not return the same way.

You have been warned.

Faerie Games

Faeries simply love to play games; the trouble is many of their games are at our expense. These games can stem from minor simple pranks and harmless fun, to games that can be far more sinister.

Fae can cross dimensions as well, which means that they can enter your dreams and seek to manipulate you through them. There are many more dimensions than most of us could ever realise even here on our own plane. The mind is a dimension entirely on its own when you write a story or draw a picture.

Fae can, if they choose you, to manipulate you and find you in any of these places.

They like dreams best, though not all Fae can cross into dreams, many can, they find it easier to hold our attention while dreaming and are more open to suggestions. Dreaming is also a direct line to our subconscious. If you do not want to interact with them in this way, then the best thing to do is to ignore them. What they want from you is a reaction, if they don't get one they will get bored and move away. By ignoring them you can avoid giving offence. Such as telling them to get lost (rude) to them anyway.

In dreams, the Fae can use trickery to get a token from you, the most common of these is asking for kisses.

What happens in a dream is very real to them, so after several kisses, they might consider you married.

Bar El

Once upon a Faerie time, a long time ago. Or maybe it was yesterday, it's often hard to know.

A young woman was divorcing her husband of seven years because of his cruelty and unfaithfulness.

She rented a cottage for the winter for herself and her son, Euan, who was four years old.

Euan liked to play in one of the outhouses close to the cottage, so after checking it out for anything dangerous and finding it looked quite safe, she allowed him to make a den here, as most little boys like to do.

One day she heard him chattering away and laughing, so smiling to herself she popped her head around the door and asked him who he was talking to.

"Bar El," he replied. After asking who Bar El was, he replied that he lived there in the shed, but he was happy to let Euan play there.

So the weeks passed, then one day she heard another voice coming from the den, going in, she was surprised to find only Euan there. After asking him who the other voice belonged to he replied, "You know who it is Mummy? I've told you. It is Bar El".

"Can I meet him?" she asked, but the little boy said he would ask, but Bar El was very shy.

That night after she had put her son to bed, she went out to the outhouse and started to search for it.

Right at the very back, smelling damp and musty, was an old apple barrel. Deciding that she could use it for storage after she had given it a good clean. She lifted it to take it outside

"Ouch!" came a little voice, "Please be careful. I haven't been moved for such a long time, I am a bit stiff".

Almost dropping it in shock, she looked closer and saw a little face in the wood, looking at her.

"Are you Bar El?" she asked, "Yes," he replied.

She carefully carried him outside where he told her that he used to live in a large forest and he had lots of friends. But one day two men came with big axes and cut his tree down. He was taken away from all of his friends and his tree was cut up and turned into lots of different things. They turned him into this strange thing and called him Bar El. Suddenly the penny dropped with her, and she realised he was trying to say 'barrel'.

He had become an apple barrel. So, the next day, her and her son, took Bar El to the woodland where he quickly found a tree without its own dryad, so he moved and lives there very happily to this day.

Visiting Faerie Land

If you have ever sat outside in the countryside, or even in your garden at dusk, and experienced a stirring inside you, a feeling that is not quite a memory, or not quite a recognition?

Nonetheless, this feeling is strong enough to create a yearning in you, then chances are high that you have previously lived a life as Fae.

In fact, you could have lived all of your past lives as Fae and this could be your very first time as a human.

We all have an incredible set of senses which not only provide us with information, but they also provide information that keeps us safe.

Smell, taste, touch, and hearing, all open the door of perception.

Our ancestors relied upon these senses and lived by them. They revered and honoured those such as Druids and Wise women who could skilfully navigate both worlds?

The Shamans of Great Britain, Magicians, and Wise women, were the healers, Astrologers, and Herbalists.

The Witch's ointment, called Ying ointment, was made by using the herbs henbane, belladonna mandrake, and Datura, or thorn apple. This ointment is known to facilitate an out-of-body experience.

This ritual is still preserved today in the children's nursery rhyme:

Ride a cock horse, to Banbury cross,

to see a fine lady upon a white horse.

With rings on her fingers,

and bells on her toes.

She will have music, wherever she goes.

The cock horse in this instance refers to a witch's broomstick on which she would fly to the Sabbat. The rings on her fingers are the ring that she was given by the King of Faerie, and the bells on her toes are a reference to her dancing ability. A witch with bells on her toes would be a high priestess.

Many of our nursery rhymes and faerie tales are direct references to the old pagan ways and left coded messages behind that only the initiated would understand.

Faerie Influence

The effects of faerie influence are very real, and perhaps the most universally significant thing about Fae as a group, is that they can manipulate you because they enjoy it. They can interfere with our perception of reality. This is not only how we see things such as glamour, but can alter how we feel. This is why the Fae are so hard to resist. I can guarantee that you will never see someone being dragged off to their land screaming and kicking, absolutely not.

You will see them dancing and jigging in ecstasy. They can make us feel blissful and enchanted, or despondent, it entirely depends on the face on their mood at the time.

Even if we might know on some level that our strings are being pulled, it would take tremendous willpower on our part to be able to pull back.

Their lure is hypnotic and they know how to play on your feelings and your emotions. This is one of the most dangerous things when you interact with them and the key word here is protection. Make sure you always have your shield in place, whenever you interact with them.

There are stories of people eating the most beautiful meal with them and being left craving more. Only for the Fae to reveal they had actually been eating soil. Then laugh and think that it was a merry jest.

Faerie influence can be so powerful that it can affect you even when they are not trying to. This is just something that they do.

It is something very raw and primal within us that makes us call to them in the very deepest recess of our soul.

Suddenly you might yearn to be by water or in the mountains or forests, this impulse will grow and grow until it has been satisfied.

You might start recalling memories, but don't know when. Or hear singing when nobody is there.

What happens if the Fae is really intending to take you away with them.

Unless you really want to go, then we are back to protection and grounding again. No matter how much I repeat it, it still won't be enough.

All of this talk of people coming and going, is simply talk.

Unless you have fake blood or a very strong protector, then the chances are once they get you there, there you will stay.

I don't know if you know the story of the milkmaid, while bringing her cows down to be milked, came upon a party of Fae men sitting by the river. They bound her with rope and took her back to their land. Then after taking her to the kitchen, told her that she was to bake bread and that once the flour bin was empty, she could go home.

Of course, the flour bin was magical, and refilled itself over and over again.

Then an old woman took pity on her. She herself had been stolen when she was a girl.

So she told her that after she had put the bread in the oven, she should scrape up the used flour that she had used to knead the bread and pour it back into the bin. This charm worked and the bin stayed empty. When the Fae saw this, they were furious because they knew it was the old woman who had betrayed them.

They had to keep their promise though and take the girl back.

No one ever discovered what happened to the old woman.

But I don't think that it would have been good.

For hundreds of years, folklore has been passed down to us, filled with dire warnings about how the Fae can't be trusted.

That is a sweeping statement and I think unfair, some Fae can be trusted up to a point anyway, but that won't stop them from trying to cheat you because getting the better of humans is in their genetics.

Some Fae can be addictive, I speak now of Elves and Sidhe, the more that you interact with them the more you will want to. You might find yourself thinking up ridiculous things, just so you can call them and ask.

At the start, they will be tolerant of this because they know perfectly well how they affect us. But after a while, they simply do not come until they are ready.

Other stories tell of people returning after hundreds of years only to find the world a changed place. They then disintegrate into a pile of dust.

However, if the situation falls on you, you will be changed and will never be the same again.

Of course, there is always the chance that you will fall madly in love with one of them and find the happy ever after. There is no way of knowing.

Fae is also well known to be possessive, remember the kisses we spoke about earlier? If this happens, they could very well find that they consider you theirs.

If a Fae takes a real shine to you and keeps bringing you gifts, this could also indicate that he considers you his. A point worth mentioning here, don't be too flattered by an excess of gifts because they will almost certainly have been stolen from someone else. And somewhere in the world, they will be looking for them.

How will you know if a Fae has claimed you?

I asked my mother how I would know when I was in labour, and her reply was, you will know.

There has been much said recently about how you should react if you are fed up with them playing games with you.

The first thing to do is not get angry. They adore this, it is the reaction they always hope for. In fact, you should go for the exact opposite and ignore them.

They want a reaction, if you don't give it, then the joke is on them. They will soon get bored and go off to find someone more fun than you.

It is also advised to learn how to apply mental blocks to protect you from their manipulation, in other places, such as work. You could also put some rules in rooms that you really don't want them going into.

The varieties of Fae you will encounter here, can be quite staggering, because Fae from all four continents will gather here and many you will never have heard of, let alone, never seen.

Think of Alice in Wonderland in terms of a very bizarre and unique face.

Fights can and often do break out, and they can become so serious that they can very quickly become wars. It is ever-changing, never constant and always moving.

It is certainly not twee with little hobbit villages all around you.

Something else to surprise you is its sheer vastness. This memory is their world and not a country.

We really only know about the Celtic Faeries here, but they are spread all over the world and are from all countries, ethnicity and colours.

Some people have actually stumbled there by mistake, although this is rare.

A Dwarf, known as the gatekeeper, stands at each portal as a guard. The dimensional gates are spaced all over the world, and they range from forests and mountains to the heart of urban cities. You could even come across one at the local tip, but you can be sure that the portal was there long before your local council decided to turn that area into a dumping ground.

This realm does carry the danger to mortals because many of them will be very happy to see you. There will always be some who aren't.

I have been to this realm three times, the first time that I went I had to call on my animal totem to get me out.

For the other two, I went with my Sidhe guide.

Having a relationship with a Fae is mostly wonderful, but they can in a way become as addictive as a drug. You feel so amazing when you are with them, that as soon as they go, you find yourself yearning to have them back. You end up thinking the most ridiculous questions, simply to call them back.

They know full well their effect on you, so at first they are amused, but this will soon fade into annoyance and they will visit only when it suits them.

There are several ways to visit this realm and by far the safest way is by invitation. If you have been invited, then you will be perfectly safe.

The other is by going through a portal.

The likelihood is that you will be safe unless they want to keep you.

One of their characteristics is that they have no respect for others.

If they want something, they really do expect to reach out their hand and take it.

The other way to visit is with a guide who agrees to take you there and bring you back.

Standing on grass, push your feet and toes deep down into the ground. Imagine roots shooting out from the soles of your feet going deep down into the Earth.

Close your eyes (you can sit on a chair doing this, if you have mobility issues)

Now see yourself standing in a beautiful meadow filled with daisies and buttercups. To your left is a thick forest, to your right is a river. You are now standing on the boundary between their realm and ours.

State your purpose out loud. If you are looking for a guide to show you the Faerie realm and keep you safe? Be specific in your needs.

Soon a small boat paddles into view, and someone steps out (this bit will be very personal to you) and tells you that they will be your guide in exchange for? (their price). At this point, thank them for coming, and tell them that you will consider their terms.

Now it is time to return home.

If their terms are more than you wish to pay, then when you return
tell them so.

They might reduce their price or they might simply leave.

If they do, then keep on repeating this process until you get a fair
bargain, and don't forget to check out any pitfalls before agreeing.

When you do reach the door of Faerie land you will be asked to take
your shoes and clothing off. You will be given a white linen robe to
wear.

Before entering, place your shoes in the doorway. Preventing the
door from closing properly. Now you are ready to have the ride of
your life. Enjoy it!

Sometimes they dance in my garden.

I can't resist a peep.

A blur of jewelled colours, spinning in a ring.

Their laughter sounds like the peel of a thousand bells.

Faerie children, with rosy cheeks and rosebuds lips,

tiny feet stamp with joy upon the earth,

and Faerie music serenades their mirth.

Faerie Children.

As the dawn creeps above the hill,

I see the children dancing still.

And soon their parents call,

"Away, Away"

And I want so much to beg them, stay.

It is time for them to go to bed,

I should, it must be said.

That I have watched them all night long.

Enchanted by a Faerie song.

Many Faerie encounters are overlooked simply because we don't recognise what we are seeing.

Yet many of these encounters provide us with a rich and rewarding experience.

I call these the presence of Faerie.

Just because we don't see them does not mean that they are not there.

Your presence is felt as energy, and your intuition becomes well defined and sharp.

This feeling is often amplified at certain times of day.

These are called the between time, and the most important one is twelve o'clock noon, and midnight. They last barely sixty seconds before they fade at just one minute past the hour, and the moment is lost.

This moment in time holds what has been described as sanctity by some, while others describe it as contentedness, euphoria and otherworldliness.

Of course, the Faerie presence is always with us, but at linear times it becomes much stronger.

We hardly would ever expect to encounter this is in busy inner cities, yet it is happening more and more, as the countryside gets built on for new housing estates and the greenery decreases. What happens to the Fae that lived there first?

The answer is nothing happened to them, they are still there. The Fae are holding on to their old ground. So now they are living in towns and cities that once long ago were countryside.

More and more children are returning home from school and insisting that they have seen little people.

Only recently one refuse collector got the fright of his life when he went to pick up a bin, and discovered a little Leprechaun sleeping on it, with a large feral cat.

Probably a Cait Sidhe.

One experience that I would like to share with you, concerns a Guy I was seeing.

We had been dating for about six weeks, when he left me and set off to walk home. We lived in such an area where buildings and a school had recently been erected but there was still quite a bit of

162

countryside about. He was walking past a cemetery on his left and a golf course on his right. There were street lights and this was how he was able to see them so clearly.

Only several yards in front of him he saw a long snaking line of little people.

They were walking in single file and led by two others riding horses. They came from the golf course and crossed the road disappearing into the graveyard.

He fled back to my home and banged on my door frantically. Dad went downstairs to open the door, and the rest of the family crowded on the landing to see what was going on?

Now remember that we were in the early days of our romance, he had met my parents no more than half a dozen times, yet here he was shaking like a leaf and telling my father he had just seen Faeries by the golf course. Not only that, but he refused to leave.

He had no idea how I would react to that, never mind my parents.

I was all for grabbing my coat and going after them, but Dad thought he was on drugs.

He slept on the sofa for the night. I had to drag the information from him, because he was so reluctant to talk about it. I believed him entirely.

Sidhe Speak on Communication

Before you can see, you must be able to hear, and before you can hear you must be able to feel.

Both of our worlds are created on music. Music is the source of all life.

You need to feel the music, and its vibration beat with your heart, then nothing will be denied to you.

Because we all manifest on different vibrations, it means that we are all at one with different genres of music.

When two beings can interact at this level and waveforms and thoughts are exchanged, we are experiencing telepathic communication.

These thought forms come on a different level than physical, so my being present to communicate with you, for us to be able to communicate together.

What we achieve in our telepathic communication requires true unity and depends on its success by us being on similar vibrations.

If you understand that your energy field is in a constant state of vibration, you will perceive that you can communicate at any time with those beings that are on a similar frequency. You have heard the saying that 'Like, attracts Like,' now you can see that this is true, like does indeed call to like.

If you should encounter a being whose vibration does not feel right to you, then you must repulse it and move away. So it is with musical forms, music also exists through vibration and so not all music will sit comfortably with you.

In Celtic lore they speak of Suantrai, Goltrai and the Geantrai, three different strains of harp music, that are used to induce sleep, healing, sorrow or joy. This goes well beyond the sound it creates, its effect is so profound because it goes way beyond our level of hearing and touches our energy field and aligns it to one of those three states that we just referred to.

Music has the same result on our psyche as hypnotism has.

You asked about the use of music in your energy work, you must first develop a greater sensitivity to the energy forms of music.

This is to ensure you create the correct vibration not just for yourself and your client.

Can you imagine a state in creation that is all on the same vibration as each other? This is what will happen when the great shake comes.

First will come a great roaring from beneath the Earth, then torrential rain and flooding will sleep over the Earth, then a mighty fire will cleanse the Earth.

This will last for fourteen days, then she will be reborn on a much higher vibration, and those whose vibrations match will be raised up.

As channeled by myself from Gunrig

Let me go with you.

Let me walk with you among,

your mountains.

Let me sleep among your glens.

Keep me in your thoughts,

when you are far from me.

Let me know your love,

It will never end.

I want to lay with you

in garden bower.

I want to wake with you,

beneath the sun.

I want to stay with you,

under the moonlight,

to feel your kisses beneath the stars.

To share my life with you,

in joy or tears.

And when my life should end,

and I must leave you.

I will keep my promise,

that my love will never end.

Bending Time

How many times have we wished that we could bend time, or even stop it for an hour or two. We often feel as if there are not enough hours in a day, or a night, when you no sooner seem to nod off before the alarm goes off.

Time though, is a construct of our perception.

You have experienced how time can seem to fly when you are having fun, and how it drags when you have little to do.

This perhaps is to oversimplify the process, but in our world it does not exist, we are proof that you do not have to live your lives governed by time or its constraints.

You can regulate how time affects you, and your world controls you. Your lives are governed by the way you perceive time. Your sleep time is governed by time.

You get up on time, you even eat according to time. But time will not exist in the new world order.

Do you remember what we discussed earlier about words, that they create your reality?

Bending time truly becomes possible when we stop using time as a goal post.

It requires you to find a place of total stillness inside of yourself.

Let us imagine that you have to be at a certain place, at a certain time.

If your perception is that time is limited, and you have not left yourself enough time to achieve it, then you will not be able to bend time. Rather than travel with the perception you will be very late, you should travel with a complete stillness, allow yourself to let that stillness become a part of you.

Do this so that the extraneous activity, such as a ticking clock or the changing of electoral numbers on a display, have no effect on you at all. All moments then become one moment. Thus, the moment that you left home, and the moment you passed your halfway point is the same.

This becomes the same moment that you stopped at traffic lights and pulled into a parking lot. All within the same moment.

When you start to experience this inner stillness and the state of being suspended in one long moment, time begins to bend around you, and you will find you can do much more in fewer clock minutes.

From this point on, time is limitless. We understand that this is not an easy task to learn. But we are often asked why time does not exist in our world and so I have told you. This might help you understand more about time travel and people who never seem to age. This can be done. Humans practice it every day. All it takes is to find that stillness.

If you are going to practice this type of time management then you start with your perception of what time is. Now time is your master, it controls you and dictates your movements.

You must first become an island, unaffected by what is going on around you, and keep that stillness within you.

Time cannot flow around you until you master this stillness.

You cannot enforce your will on time and neither can you rule it.

When it finally stretches around you, it is responding to what you feel and not what you think.

Gunrig

Gunrig's Latest Message

We knew when the Elven Arriea fell from the sky, that the time would come when you forgot us.

It was your destiny, yet we still grieved for you.

We felt the separation deeply and many of us grieved for we lost family and friends when the separation came.

We have seen you struggle when the great darkness fell and shrouded us from each other. Yet we never forgot you as you so quickly forgot us.

We have walked at your side for many years now, but despite our efforts your eyes and ears remained closed.

The Glyph of the Silver Moon was unearthed under a tumulus by a great Shamanist teacher and the darkness began to lift.

Soon we were able to see through the darkness and as it continues to lift, you have started to recognise us again and start to remember your ancient past and our shared history.

Let me tell you the ancient ways of our peoples.

We belong to an ancient world order that witnesses Atlantis fall. We are older than the floods and ice. We belong to a place and a time when Earth was a star and the Cosmos was young.

We planted the tree of life on the Earth and wrote the names of the tribes upon the branches.

Once upon this planet there existed a land named Lemuria.

This was a good place, they wore blue robes on their bodies and decorated their skin with stars to remind them that we all came from the stars and that we should never forget where our origins are.

The elders sang to the crystals and the more that they sang, the more the power of the crystal grew.

They sang so that the crystals would remember us through all time.

There are thirteen glyphs buried within what is called Wales, ten have been recovered and the crystals have remembered.

Many millennia have passed while these glyphs have remained hidden, but now they are singing again calling to their lost brothers.

When the last three glyphs are recovered, then the prophecy will be fulfilled and the world that you know will be no more. Instead a new reign will commence and a new world order.

The time of wars will be over, greed and hatred will be no more, we will heal illness by a touch and the seas will be clear and blue.

This will all be achieved by all of us allowing our vibration to be compatible once more with all the tribes that will live here.

The Elivae search for the glyphs, and some have even heard them singing in the hills.

There will be those among the human race that will become keystones of the new Earth.

172

All nations will be fairly seated at the council and they will not be chosen by the criteria in place today.

Some of you have already been chosen while others remain under observation.

Energy bodies will alter and you too will be called the shining ones. Those willing to prepare you for the initiations have already arrived on your Earth and are moving amongst you.

We ask that you respond to this challenge and open your hearts and minds to the experiences to come.

We, your kin, rejoice that soon our separation will be over and our peoples united once more.

Gunrig. As channeled by me.

The Power of Names

Once upon a time there was a poor miller who had a beautiful daughter. One day he foolishly boasted that she could spin straw into gold. The king heard of this, and sending for her, he locked her in a room filled with straw and a spinning wheel. Telling her that if she failed to spin every single piece into gold, then he would execute her.

The poor girl was beside herself and try as hard as she could, she could not turn straw into gold. As dawn made its approach, a strange little man appeared. He promised to spin the straw into gold for her, if she promised to give him something precious.

He asked for the first-born child and the desperate the girl agreed. She married the King and eventually a baby was born.

The queen had almost forgotten her promise to the strange little man, but suddenly he appeared and told her he had come to claim the baby.

The queen begged and she pleaded until at last he told her that if she could guess his name, then she could keep her baby.

After failing to guess his name twice, she knew she only had one try left. She went walking in the forest when she suddenly saw the smoke from a fire and dancing around it was the strange little man. He was singing a song to himself "For shame, for, she will never guess my name, for I am Rumpelstiltskin!"

The next night he arrived and the queen called out that Rumpelstiltskin is your name. The strange man went purple, then disappeared in a puff of smoke.

To name something is to define it and an attempt to set limits on it. Even personal names can seek to define us or categorise us.

You should also keep in mind that you did not name yourselves, your parents named you. Personal names are insignificant when you think that over many lifetimes you will have lived with many names.

Despite this, not one of the names that you have been given are remotely correct. Not one of them will truly resonate with the note you received at the time of your first birth.

Though we are all connected at a spirit level, each individual emanation of spirit has a signature that defines it.

Bright Peace the Goblin

I wrote this story when I was thirteen years old, for my much younger brother, who was in bed with mumps. Unfortunately, I was only half way through it when he interrupted me, saying, "If I promise to be very, very good, will you stop reading it!"

I hope that it gets a better reception from you!

Once upon a Faerie time a long time ago, or maybe it was yesterday, sometimes it's hard to know, A goblin whose name was Bright Peace, (nobody in Faerieland really understood how he got this name) because Bright Peace was really not very bright and neither were things very peaceful whenever he was around, but I digress.

Bright Peace was ambling along this sunny country lane looking for Blackberries, when he heard the clip, clip, clop, of old Jasper, farmer Brown's faithful old horse, who pulled his cart.

Remembering the last time, he and the farmer met and had threatened to shoot him, Bright Peace dived into the long grass and prudently waited for the good farmer to pass.

Now Bright Peace had set out that day with all good intentions, intent on not going near the farmers house, but just as he passed close to Bright Peace, hiding a voice, definitely not the farmers, called out, "Give us a kiss then!"

Bright Piece's ears shot up. Who on Earth, thought the goblin, would say that!

Farmers do go to bed early, because they have to get up early, and this, dear reader, was the first bit of luck our goblin had had in a long time.

Because he was a regular to the farmers house, Bright Peace knew that a small window in the pantry was easy to climb through.

Climbing in, our goblins nose began to twitch, he was picking up an unidentified smell that he had never come across before.

Following his twitching nose, he came to the parlour where our farmer and his lady wife took their ease. Two battered, but comfortable armchairs, where the Browns took their ease.

Hanging from the ceiling was a cage, and when our goblin peered in he jumped back in shock. Something with very beady eyes looked back at him.

"Give us a kiss," it shrieked at our goblin, Bright Peace shuddered at the very thought.

"Certainly not," he replied.

Reaching up and grabbing the cage, he climbed out of the pantry window and took his stolen goods back with him to the land of Elfinfae.

Today was the Faerie Queen's birthday, and now he had a gift for her.

Bursting through the palace doors, a party was in progress. Old father Pelligrew, with his family of Leprechauns was there, along with the Greypikes, drunk on honey wine already.

In fact, everyone who was anyone in the land of elfin faces was there.

Bright Peace pushed through the throng of preening Faeries and knelt at the Faerie Queene's feet. "A gift for you, your majesty," handing his package to her.

Suddenly the queen screamed and dropped the gift, the cage door flew open and out flew poll, dive bombing everyone.

The Faeries yelled and dived under the tables for cover, all except for old father Pettigrew, who whipped off a tablecloth and proceeded to shake it at pol, shouting "Olé".

He had once been to Spain.

Poll sat up in the rafters and peered myopically down at the scene below.

"What on earth is it?" asked the Queen, looking very angry at Bright Peace.

Just then one of the queen's councillors stepped forward.

"If it pleases your majesty," he said "It is a magician from foreign lands".

"What does it want?" asked the queen.

"We will have to parley with it" replied her councillors wisely.

So right there and then, everyone who was at the queen's birthday party, took up the negotiating position. (this involved sitting cross legged on the floor) And it was from this position that they all looked up at poll, who of course looked down at them.

Clearing his throat and feeling very important, the queen's councillor asked the poll, what he wanted?

"Give us a kiss," screeched poll, "Go on pretty boy, give old poll a kiss".

The counsellor nearly fainted with shock.

"Kiss it you fool," shrieked the queen, who was now bright red with rage.

So, with trembling knees the poor old councillor flew up into the rafters and prepared to kiss poll.

Poll on the other hand, was intrigued with these proceedings and watched intently, that is until the councillor puckering up planted a large kiss on polls head.

Everyone watched as completing his mission, the counsellor very quickly resumed his place on the floor.

It was at this point that a human boy entered the hall with a tray of hazel nuts. This was more to Polls liking than whatever it was that strange creature had planted on his head. So Poll dive bombed the hazel nuts and came to rest on the silver tray and spat nut shells at everyone.

Well, "If it isn't our old poll,"

"You know this magician?" queried the queen.

"He isn't a magician", the boy said. Whose name was Tom, "He is a parrot, my father brought back from a faraway place."

Poll recognised his voice and gave a very loud squawk in recognition, "If it's yours, then you may take it away," cried the queen.

And so, the doors to Faerieland were thrown open, and Tom, with Poll sitting on his head, returned home, where there was much rejoicing.

Bright Peace however was a different story. He was sentenced to two years on the treadmill.

Once he was released, he married Olga the Ogre's daughter. She had three eyes, one blue, one brown, and one green, and she always kept at least one of them on him.

And it's here we must end it my friends.

I hope sincerely that you have enjoyed our walk in the Dark Wood.

Until we meet again, I wish you all health, wealth and love.

MAB

Printed in Great Britain
by Amazon

82516936R00108